DISCARD

Jossey–Bass Teacher

Jossey-Bass Teacher provides educators with practical knowledge and tools to create a positive and lifelong impact on student learning. We offer classroom-tested and research-based teaching resources for a variety of grade levels and subject areas. Whether you are an aspiring, new, or veteran teacher, we want to help you make every teaching day your best.

From ready-to-use classroom activities to the latest teaching framework, our value-packed books provide insightful, practical, and comprehensive materials on the topics that matter most to K–12 teachers. We hope to become your trusted source for the best ideas from the most experienced and respected experts in the field.

Praise for the Frostig Center and
The Six Success Factors for Children with Learning Disabilities

"Educators desperately want to help their students to achieve success, but they cannot identify or isolate the specific skills and attributes that the child will need in this journey. Enter California's renowned Frostig Center. This extraordinary organization has conducted research on successful individuals with learning disabilities and the results have been invaluable to parents and educators.

"[This book] provides educators, parents, and other caregivers with pragmatic and measurable strategies to foster maturity and independence for youth with learning problems. The activities demonstrate that success is not amorphous and unattainable—rather, it can be achieved by adopting an established set of behaviors, attitudes, and characteristics. These activities will be enormously useful as you prepare your students for their journey to adulthood."

—From the foreword by Richard D. Lavoie, bestselling author, *It's So Much Work to be Your Friend* and *The Motivation Breakthrough*

"These activities will help your students be confident, successful, and able to partner with you to overcome the challenges of their disabilities."

—Dale S. Brown, senior manager, LD OnLine (ldonline.org)

"Over 20 years of research support the development of this remarkable book. Written to equip teachers with lessons designed to help students with learning differences be empowered for life, the Frostig Center has made a substantial contribution to education. The lesson plans for teaching strategies in goal-setting, perseverance, emotional coping, proactivity, and developing social support systems are accessible and applicable in a variety of settings. This will be required reading in our program."

—Debrah Hall, Ph.D. program director, The Monarch School, Houston, Texas

The 6 Success Factors for Children with Learning Disabilities

Ready-to-Use Activities to Help Kids with LD Succeed in School and in Life

The Frostig Center Educators

Foreword by Richard D. Lavoie

JOSSEY-BASS
A Wiley Imprint
www.josseybass.com

Published by Jossey-Bass.
A Wiley Imprint
989 Market Street, San Francisco, CA 94103-1741 — www.josseybass.com

Jossey-Bass books and products are available through most bookstores. To contact Jossey-Bass directly, call our Customer Care Department within the U.S. at 800-956-7739, outside the U.S. at 317-572-3986, or fax 317-572-4002.

Jossey-Bass also publishes its books in a variety of electronic formats. Some content that appears in print may not be available in electronic books.

Library of Congress Cataloging-in-Publication Data

The six success factors for children with learning disabilities : ready-to-use activities to help kids with LD succeed in school and in life / the Frostig Center.
    p. cm. – (Jossey-Bass teacher)
  Includes bibliographical references.
  ISBN 978-0-470-38377-3 (alk. paper)
  1. Learning disabled children–Education. 2. Special education–Activity programs. 3. Learning disabled children–Life skills guides. I. Marianne Frostig Center of Educational Therapy.
  LC4704.S57 2009
  371.9–dc22
                                             2008046218

Printed in the United States of America
FIRST EDITION
PB Printing   10 9 8 7 6 5 4 3 2 1

Contents

Contents   **vii**

About This Book

When a group of students is gathered to learn, a subset of them will struggle with academics in ways different from the majority; some of the these may be considered to have a learning disability. The teacher of this group senses intuitively that those most challenged students will accomplish wonderful things: invent lifesaving devices, create noble companies, and help humanity. Nevertheless, the teacher needs tools to move those students in these lofty directions. The collection of activities and resources in this book will aim the different learners toward success life.

The lessons in this book address the six attributes that have been identified by highly successful adults with learning disabilities as those qualities that helped them be successful. These Success Attributes are self-awareness (recognizing strengths and weaknesses and compartmentalizing disabilities), proactivity (engaging in the world actively), perseverance (pursuing a goal despite adversity), goal setting (establishing step-by-step processes to accomplishment), social support systems (seeking and accepting help from others), and emotional coping strategies (recognizing and premeditating stress).

This book also contains advice on how to expand existing lessons and create new ones. The lessons are adaptable to a wide range of development and academic levels, time lines, and experiences. Once educators gain familiarity and comfort with the success attributes set out in this book through working with their students and the lessons contained in this book, the attributes will become an integral part of their teaching practice, expanding their own—and their students'—opportunities for success.

Foreword

Several years ago, a group of Japanese and American researchers conducted extensive surveys with parents in their respective countries. The research was designed to compare and contrast the parental attitudes and behaviors of Japanese and American families. When the results were announced, the American media became obsessed with the findings, which were widely published and discussed.

The press focused particularly on the responses to the question: *What is your greatest wish for your child when s/he grows up?* The overwhelming number of American parents responded, "We want our kids to be *happy.*" The overwhelming number of Japanese parents responded, "We want our kids to be *productive.*" The media cited these responses as reflective of the wide diversity between Japanese parenting and American parenting.

I did not agree with this assessment. In fact, I felt that the responses reflected the universality of parenthood. Both sets of parents were saying the same thing: to be happy, a person must be productive, and to be productive, a person must be happy. Quite simply, a well-adjusted adult must have a reason to get out of bed in the morning. He must arise with the belief that if he doesn't get out of bed, the world will be diminished in some way. This feeling of belonging and productivity is the motivational drive that propels most functioning and mature adults to learn, work, and grow.

Basically the parents responding to the surveys were saying that they wanted their children to be *successful.* Of course, success, like beauty, is in the eye of the beholder. A seventeen-year-old's announcement that she plans to join the circus would come as a crushing blow to a parent who is a clinical neurobiologist but would be welcome news for a parent who is a fifth-generation trapeze performer. "Success" can be an amorphous and puzzling concept.

Nevertheless, there are some attributes that are generally accepted as reflective of a successful life. Among these are:

- Fulfilling leisure activities
- Positive peer relationships
- Meaningful employment
- Physical and mental well-being
- High self-esteem
- Financial security
- Close family ties
- Community membership

These goals offer particular challenges to children with learning disabilities, as well as to their teachers. If you examine these goals, you recognize that they require the specific skills that are often lacking in these children. Students with learning problems have significant difficulty in planning, prioritizing, persevering, and participating. Their language and learning problems create obstacles to their success.

Educators are often frustrated by this challenge. They desperately want to help their students to achieve this elusive "success," but they cannot identify or isolate the specific skills and attributes that a particular child will need in this journey. Enter California's renowned Frostig Center. This extraordinary organization has conducted research on successful individuals with learning disabilities, and the results have been invaluable to parents and educators guiding youth with learning problems.

The magic of this project lies in the research design that Frostig used when conducting this study. For many years, researchers have examined learning disabled adults who were unemployed, underemployed, and nonproductive. Through these studies, the researchers hoped to determine what these failing adults did *wrong*.

The Frostig research team took a different approach: they chose to examine and survey a group of successful, productive learning disabled adults in order to determine what those folks did *right*. What were the attributes, behaviors, and characteristics that contributed to their success? This intensive, brilliantly designed examination identified six traits that were common to the successful adults and clearly contributed to their success and growth. These traits and behaviors had a positive impact on these individuals' progress, performance, and development. The implication of Frostig's research is clear: these traits and behaviors contributed significantly to the success of these individuals; therefore parents and educators should promote and foster these traits in children to ensure their successful adjustment into adulthood.

The parents and teachers of youngsters with learning disorders often view their children's future with trepidation and anxiety. What does the future hold? Can he function as an independent, autonomous adult? Will her learning challenges continue to hold her back and diminish her potential? These questions are valid and understandable. However, it is also important that parents and teachers consistently communicate faith and optimism for a child's future. The child needs to know that the future holds good and great things for him or her.

I was counseling an adolescent with special needs and asked if he had discussed his postgraduation plans with his parents. "No," he responded. "My mom and dad never discuss my future. I think that they are afraid of it."

The student's insightful comment caused me to reflect on my interactions with my own children. My wife and I are blessed with three competent and confident children who thrived in school. Countless times Janet and I sent subtle (and often unintentional) messages to them that we had great confidence in their future. Comments like, "When you go to college ... ," "When you have your own kids ... ," and "When you have a house of your own," sent clear parental messages that their futures were bright.

As a teacher of students with special needs, how often do you hear such comments? How often do you let your students know that their future will offer excitement, fulfillment, and satisfaction? If students feel that *you* are excited about their future, they will soon develop this optimism as well.

The Frostig Center has done much to carry on the legacy of its founder, Dr. Marianne Frostig. The center has contributed significantly to the knowledge base of the learning disabilities field and has made a profound difference in the lives of thousands of children through the direct educational services that it provides. But when the history of the Frostig Center is written, I feel that the Success Attributes project may well be its crowning work.

The book in your hands offers invaluable data and information related to the Success Attributes. It provides educators, parents, and other caregivers with pragmatic and measurable strategies to foster maturity and independence for youth with learning problems. The activities in this book demonstrate that success is not amorphous and unattainable. Rather, it can be achieved by adopting an established set of behaviors, attitudes, and characteristics. These activities will be enormously useful as you prepare your students for their journey to adulthood.

It really is simple: adhere to the success attributes, and you will be successful. Simple? Yes. Easy? No. Adopting and embracing these traits is hard work and will require concentrated effort from all parties, but the end is well worth this work. I commend the Frostig educators for their tireless efforts in completing this project. The field—and countless families—are in their debt. They have provided us with a compass and a road map for the challenging journey that lies ahead. Bon voyage and Godspeed!

Richard D. Lavoie, M.A., M.Ed.
Author of *It's So Much Work to Be Your Friend*
and *The Motivation Breakthrough*

Barnstable, MA
March 2009

About the Frostig Center

The Frostig Center in Pasadena, California, was founded by Dr. Marianne Frostig in the early 1950s to serve students with learning disabilities. As with any other organization, numerous changes have taken place since its inception; nevertheless, three key concepts continue to remain intact and provide a guiding force for the center.

The first is Dr. Frostig's belief that the center should serve the whole child. On a daily basis, this means that each student's academic, physical, social, and emotional needs have equal concern to the staff. Consequently, the center's staff devotes extra time to help and stimulate areas of child development in addition to academic preparation. The second concept is that the center's staff functions as an interdisciplinary team. As a result, teachers, teaching assistants, speech/language therapists, counselors, and educational therapists all have important and equal input into the decision-making process.

Finally, what drives the philosophy of the center is its three-part mission. The center directly serves students with learning disabilities through the school and tutoring programs. It provides professional development opportunities in differentiated instruction for special and general educators outside the school. Finally, Frostig's research department conducts research studies related to learning disabilities both on-site and in the surrounding community.

To learn more about the Frostig Center, please go to www.frostig.org.

The Contributors

A number of staff from the Frostig Center contributed to this book. These professionals brought their lessons to meetings for others to critique and designed lesson plans to better teach the Success Attributes. Their support was essential to this project.

In alphabetical order, the contributors are Heather Chatem, master teacher; Lowry Ewig, speech and language therapist; Lee Fox, lead teacher; Roberta Goldberg, director of community outreach; Monica Gomez, social skills coordinator; Janet Huynh, teaching assistant; Olga Jerman, director of research; Jacqueline Knight, master teacher; Andrea Lombardi, senior educational specialist; Marianne Manuel, teaching assistant; Helen Overstreet, librarian; Beverlee Paine, senior educational specialist; Chris Schnieders, director of teacher training; Toni Shahak, speech and language therapist; and Heather Sweeney, teaching assistant.

Acknowledgments

As the Introduction to this book indicates, the professionals who were involved in it are numerous and span about half of the history of the Frostig Center. Historically speaking, gratitude is owed to Mary Oi and Dr. Frostig who began the initial conversation and organization which resulted in this work. Thanks to Nancy Spekman, Marshall Raskind, and Eleanor Higgins, who served as directors of research at different times and carried forward the study that resulted in the Success Attributes. Appreciation to Ken Herman and Roberta Goldberg, who served on the Research Committee during the data collection of the study. The contribution of these professionals changed the lives of individuals with learning disabilities forever.

Gratitude is expressed to past teachers and therapists who implemented the first lesson plans to teach the Success Attributes. This sequentially leads to acknowledging the countless students who have had the opportunity to participate in all of the work from the beginning research through the interviews, to the efficacy study subject.

Thanks go to Bennett Ross, the executive director of the center, whose commitment, support, and encouragement throughout the Success Attributes years led to the creation of this book. He provided the leadership with the help of his managers: Chris Schnieders, director of teacher training; Roberta Goldberg, director of community outreach; Olga Jerman, director of research; Tobey Shaw, principal; Bruce Hirsch, director of clinical services; Kaye Sargeant, director of finance; and Rosemarie Boerger, director of development.

Coordinating a project this complex—involving multiple views, personalities, and myriad details—would seem impossible to a mere human. Fortunately for this work, Susie Hartley, an administrative research assistant with superpowers, accepted her role to organize, arrange, and edit with speed and grace. Her willingness, cooperation, and talents are greatly valued. Additionally, Chris Schnieders headed the collaborating, writing, and editing of the professional team.

While the contributors were designing the book, work at the center continued. To all of the students, teachers, teaching assistants, therapists, professional developers, and support staff, we, the book contributors, are appreciative.

Introduction

Two federal underfunded mandates occupy a considerable amount of the time that today's educators spend planning and implementing school curriculum. No Child Left Behind legislation drives academic planning and curricular decisions aimed at improving the performance of all students in academic areas. The Individuals with Disabilities Education Act has slightly less impact on these areas, but it also requires that general and special educators make curriculum accessible to all learners, with the expectation that everyone can succeed. Both laws are important, but as the regulations are implemented, school personnel are realizing that this drive to one-size-fits-all academics may not be sufficient for the whole spectrum of learners. Thus, many educators are looking for ways to educate students for their own individual success, which at times may differ from system requirements.

Dropout rates are rising. School officials across the country are calling for more personalized approaches to education, including smaller schools and alternatives to traditional curriculum. Therefore, a curriculum that connects to students and provides practice and strategies to be successful might help fill an ever-widening gap between the interests of students and schools' expectations.

Teachers are clamoring for tools and activities to use with students who struggle to learn or are labeled with learning disabilities. They need materials that will promote these students' overall growth and move them toward a brighter future. With the increase in inclusion in general education, both special and general education teachers need a variety of ideas and activities to integrate into the content areas. They want strategies that they can teach students to use throughout their lives.

The Frostig Center, Success, and Learning Disabilities

This book is a collection of lesson plans and activities that were developed over the years in our attempts to foster success in students at the Frostig School. Success is not easy to define; it means different things to different people and may even mean something different at different times in a person's life. Although views of success vary, there appear to be a number of things that most people point to when they think of success: good friends, positive family relations, being loved, self-approval, job satisfaction, physical and mental health, financial comfort, spiritual contentment, and an overall sense of meaning in one's life. Different individuals place lesser or greater emphasis on these various components of success. As educators, we hope that we can help our students not only to achieve academically but also to achieve a satisfying and rewarding life. How do we do this? Research at the Frostig Center has provided some insight and some answers.

Frostig Research and the Success Attributes

This collection of activities is based on a twenty-year longitudinal research project conducted by the Frostig Center that traced the lives of a group of former students who attended the center between 1968 and 1975. The purpose of the study was to identify factors that led to positive life outcomes in persons with learning disabilities.

The Frostig researchers believed that identifying these factors and then fostering them would be of tremendous value in helping students with learning disabilities reach their full potential and lead satisfying and rewarding lives. In addition, the research team sought to understand why, despite similar backgrounds and learning difficulties, some of the students ended up as happy, satisfied, and productive members of society, whereas others were barely able to keep their heads above water emotionally, socially, and financially. In an effort to gain such understanding, the research team initiated first a ten-year and then a twenty-year follow-up study designed to identify various factors that led some students to "success" and others to "failure."

The ten-year follow-up study focused on identifying the internal factors and external events in the lives of the study participants when they were young adults (eighteen to twenty-two years of age) that discriminated between those who were "successful" and those who were not (Spekman, Goldberg, & Herman, 1992). Participants were identified as "successful" or "unsuccessful" using a multidimensional definition of success that included employment, education, independent living, family relations, social relationships, crime and substance abuse, life satisfaction, and physical and psychological health. Data were collected from interviews, standardized testing, and educational, psychological, and medical records. A quantitative analysis of the data revealed few meaningful, statistically significant differences between the successful and unsuccessful groups based on background-independent variables (age, gender, family socioeconomic status, ethnicity, birth order, number of siblings, IQ, diagnostic category, or services received at Frostig), cognitive measures, and academic achievement. It was concluded that success might have been related to other factors in the lives of these individuals.

A qualitative analysis proved to be more fruitful in revealing a set of what we call Success Attributes that differentiated the two groups, with the successful group illustrating greater *self-awareness* (self-acceptance of the learning disability), *proactivity*, *perseverance*, appropriate *goal setting*, the presence and use of *effective social support systems*, and *emotional coping strategies*. Further exploration of these attributes became a key goal of the twenty-year follow-up when the study participants were twenty-eight to thirty-five years old. Again, the initial quantitative analysis revealed no statistically significant differences on background variables between the successful and unsuccessful groups. A series of analyses showed that the Success Attributes were highly predictive of achieving life success when compared to such factors as academic achievement, gender, socioeconomic status, ethnicity, and even IQ. This is not to say that these factors do not have a substantial impact on the life outcomes of persons with learning disabilities, but rather that research data have shown that these attributes may play an even greater role on these individuals' lives. No doubt factors like extreme poverty or severe psychiatric problems can have a profound affect on someone's life and negate the positive influence of the Success Attributes.

Although statistical analyses were immensely valuable and provided a springboard from which interventions that promote life success could be designed, Frostig researchers hoped to get a deeper and richer understanding of the Success Attributes. They conducted another qualitative analysis that focused on the insider's perspective, that is, what the study participants had to say in their own words about living with learning disabilities. A detailed analysis of the interview transcripts provided such an understanding and has been reported in another study (Goldberg, Higgins, Raskind, & Herman, 2003).

For several years, Frostig psychologists cotaught lessons on Success Attributes with the teachers. Then the program was integrated into classes. The content of this book is adapted from lessons that have been field-tested widely by both teachers and therapists. Some of the lessons were included in an efficacy study that was conducted at the Frostig School in spring 2007 and tested the possibility of fostering future success by teaching Success Attributes. The study focused on teaching two attributes: self-awareness and goal setting. It was successful and proved that students could improve their goal-setting skills, although more research is needed to see whether these improvements are long-lasting.

How This Book Is Organized

There are six chapters in the book, each containing ten lesson plans. The lesson plans consist of an activity page that may be reproduced and distributed to students or used on an overhead projector—teaching instructions precede each activity page. Each of the six chapters addresses a specific Success Attribute. Consequently, the primary theme or focus of the lessons in the chapter is devoted to that Success Attribute. Nevertheless, themes and Success Attributes in the lessons often overlap; an activity that helps students develop strategies when they are frustrated with friends, for example, may involve both emotional coping strategies and social support systems. Drawing attention to the interconnection of the Success Attributes is important for the students' understanding and for their ability to apply and use this understanding over time. The chapters are arranged in the order that the Success Attributes were reported in the research findings. Nonetheless, the decisions about which attribute should be presented first is completely the teacher's prerogative and is dependent on individual circumstances.

Appendix A contains lists of materials, books, and movies to use with the activities. This material is extensive but not exhaustive. After teachers review the suggestions, other possibilities may come to mind that are a better match with a particular group of students. In addition to direct classroom resources, a list of related professional materials is available. Appendix B offers a number of checklists that can be used as different means of assessment: a teacher may wish to track the class's progress through the Success Attributes or rate each student's skills within the attributes to get a sense of future planning. At the same time, students may assess their individual progress with the attributes.

How to Use This Book

The lessons in this book maintain a similar format throughout. A lesson designated as an introductory lesson requires little or no prior mastery and knowledge of the terms related to Success Attributes. The intermediate lessons require some comprehension of the concepts and attribute terms, and the advanced lessons involve working with more than one Success Attribute. The objectives for each lesson derived from the initial study of the Success Attributes.

Materials are required for most of the lessons include only photocopies of the worksheets for each student and pens or pencils. Teachers may find that an overhead transparency of the student worksheet is useful to help students focus on the instruction. Once the worksheets are completed, students occasionally may construct collages or other visual representations of their work. Those activities involve arts and crafts materials such as glue, magazines for pictures, markers, and poster paper. The time required to complete each lesson is approximate and depends on the teacher's familiarity with the content and the students' language, reading, and vocabulary proficiency.

The teaching instructions that precede each activity are a combination of directions for the teacher and suggestions to provide to the students. Many of the directions for students are repeated as instructions on the reproducible worksheets. The intent of the lesson plan is to provide a structure. Teachers, however, are encouraged to create anticipatory sets, provide additional scenarios based on current happenings, and allow additional activities like role playing, expanded writing, and more collage making to increase the involvement of students in the material. The teacher is welcomed to match his or her style with the contents of the book.

For lessons that apply to more than one Success Attribute, cross-references at the top of the teaching instruction pages indicate which attributes are taught within the activity. Teachers may wish to consider whether a discussion of the other attributes is necessary prior to teaching the activity. Another alternative might be to reference a past activity when the new attribute is introduced. As students become more familiar with the attributes, the teacher should encourage discussion of the relationship among the attributes.

The suggested grade levels are flexible. Some secondary students may find some of the vocabulary simple. Some elementary students may report that talking about careers, the future, or job seeking is unrelated to their current world. The teacher using this book will have the best idea about how to connect the content of the activities with the class level of interest. When considering a lesson plan for a group of students, consider both the suggested grade level and the suggested modifications to get a general idea about possible adaptations for diverse groups. Following the section on suggested modifications are caveats related to subject sensitivity. Some students with learning disabilities have emotional issues that interfere with learning and may need special consideration during these highly personalized activities. Caveats for each lesson are mentioned for consideration.

Most of the lessons can be done independently of one another. Some of the lessons are arranged such that the follow-up lessons are paired with their initial lesson. Each chapter starts with a lesson that introduces the Success Attributes and the related terms and concepts. A teacher may either instruct students using that lesson or use that information as a basis for the next group of lessons. Several activities represent variations on a theme (for instance, students interviewing each other). These repeated experiences are deliberate to allow multiple practices. A teacher may also find that teaching a couple of lessons from one chapter and then moving to the next chapter is helpful and allows students to understand the scope of the Success Attributes. A teacher might also find that teaching similar lessons at different points throughout the year is a good way to assess students' progress with the attributes. Maintaining students' work over time will allow teachers to assess and reflect on students' progress. Using past work and perspectives may be a good starting point for current thoughts.

As a teacher becomes acquainted and comfortable with the Success Attributes, the use of vocabulary related to the attributes could be infused into the classroom. As such, the teacher will be aware of teachable moments to reinforce the formal instruction. For instance, a student who has some knowledge of proactivity and is asking a clarifying question about homework or who calls a peer for an assignment has begun to generalize proactivity to his or her own life.

In addition, many of the activities (and other related ideas that would result after teaching the lesson) can be integrated into the traditional academic curriculum. Students might graph the data from the conducted surveys, followed by a written analysis of the results. The worksheets have limited space for response, and students can expand many of their responses into paragraph or essay forms. The books or assignments used to teach goal setting can readily be selected from the academic curriculum of the program, although it might take additional planning on the part of the teacher to schedule the reading or assignment at the point where the Success Attribute has been introduced.

Several of the activities in each chapter look directly at job-seeking skills. The aim to encourage employment for students with learning disabilities is lofty and filled with a need for repeated attempts, parent involvement, and loads of denial. Older students may or may not be willing to see the purpose of practicing the lessons related to careers. Practicing those skills with younger students might be a more positive experience since sometimes they might be eager to grow up.

Who This Book Is For

The majority of the activities in this book are suitable for students in grades 3 through 12. Most of the lessons, however, are highly flexible and adaptable to a wide range of developmental levels. Both general and special educators should find the book helpful and effective in fostering Success Attributes in their students. Professionals who are engaged in collaborative settings (special and general educators working together in the same classroom) should find the activities helpful when programming for an entire class of diverse learners.

At the secondary level, content-area teachers in language arts can infuse the activities into writing assignments. School counselors can use the materials in small groups or individually with the students who are at risk for school failure. Social science teachers can use the activities while studying biographies of historical figures who demonstrate specific Success Attributes (use of support systems, goal setting, and proactivity, for example). Any teacher at the secondary level focusing on career development should appreciate this book. In special education, teachers in the field of career development and transition will find the activities of great value.

Directors of offices for students with disabilities on college campuses may also find the book a valuable resource in their advising efforts. Many times, offices of disabilities focus on providing extended timed tests and quiet or isolated places for examinations. This book may provide expanded opportunities to practice and develop strategies that focus on overall life success.

Tutors or educational therapists or psychologists who work with students individually may find the activities helpful for specific students. Parents who home-school or simply have concerns about the socioemotional needs of their children should find the book very helpful when talking about strategies related to success.

chapter one
SELF-AWARENESS

Students who are self-aware:

- Refer to themselves as "learning disabled"
- Are open about their difficulties
- Describe life events in terms of their learning disabilities, yet are not overly defined by their difficulties
- Are able to compartmentalize their disability as only one aspect of self
- Accept their learning disability
- Use appropriate services to overcome difficulties when possible
- Have a clear picture of their individual strengths and weaknesses
- Recognize and accept talents along with limitations

Introduction to Self-Awareness

Success Attribute Covered	Self-Awareness
Familiarity with Success Attributes	Introductory lesson
Suggested Grade Levels	Grades 3 to 12
Objectives	To define and identify concepts related to self-awareness
Materials Needed	Worksheet for each student Pens and pencils Chalkboard or display board for teacher notes
Approximate Time	50 minutes
Directions to Implement the Activity	Explain that the class will be working with the Success Attributes; may want to explain the research (see the Introduction to this book) Define *self-awareness, strengths and weaknesses, interests, passions,* and *compartmentalization* Ask students to identify areas of strengths and weaknesses (domains might include physical, academic, social, emotional, arts) Discuss the importance of knowing strengths and weaknesses to help select a career, work with groups, help make correct choices, being honest with self; may involve others' perceptions of individuals Ask students to summarize on the worksheet, individually, in pairs, or as a class, what was discussed in class

Suggested Modifications	Assist students with writing notes:
	
	    May need to discuss with student individually to check for understanding
	
	If the class works well together, spend time defining confidentiality for group:
	
	    What is discussed or identified as a strength or weakness by an individual stays in this room
	
	If the group has difficulty supporting one another, introduce the concepts of strengths and weaknesses in general without asking for volunteers:
	
	    Use a predetermined list of strengths and weaknesses

Caveats Regarding Possible Sensitivity of Topic	Students and/or parents can have difficulty accepting the disability, so preteaching (or a letter sent home—or both) may be needed)
	May need to inform parents before this project begins; may have to work with students individually
	May need to modify lesson to focus on strengths and weaknesses without discussing disabilities
	If discussion of disabilities is included, spending time defining disability categories for each student and discussing confidentiality among students is important

Introduction to Self-Awareness

Directions: Please take notes during the class discussion on self-awareness about what is important.

1. The Success Attributes are:

   _____   _____   _____

   _____   _____   _____

2. Define in your own words:

   a. *strengths* _____

   b. *weaknesses* _____

   c. *interests* _____

   d. *passions* _____

3. List some areas to consider when thinking about strengths and weaknesses.

   _____

   _____

4. List some reasons that it is important to know your strengths and weaknesses.

   _____

   _____

5. To be *self-aware* means:

   _____

   _____

6. *Compartmentalize* means:

   _____

   _____

7. Summarize what was discussed in class.

   _____

   _____

   _____

   _____

Rating Yourself

Success Attribute Covered	Self-Awareness
Familiarity with Success Attributes	Introductory lesson Can be used as a pretest or posttest to determine changes over the year
Suggested Grade Level	Grades 3 to 12
Objective(s)	To recognize and accept talents along with limitations
Materials Needed	Rating worksheet for each student Pencils, ruler, or highlighters (to assist with tracking)
Approximate Time	40 minutes

Directions to Implement the Activity	Introduce or review concept of self-awareness:
	
	    Successful people understand what they can do well, when they need help, why they do some things poorly
	    Understanding self is important for determining what to do in life, to select and accomplish goals
	
	Ask students to circle the number by each skill that best represents their estimation of how well they do in that area; define ratings, if needed
	
	Monitor room when students are working to assist with reading, defining terms
	
	When students have completed their individual ratings, they are paired with a classmate in order to share their findings

Suggested Modifications	Students may need help reading the skill areas Using rulers will help students mark their answers on the correct line
Caveats Regarding Possible Sensitivity of Topic	Teacher may want to review topics represented to check for individual sensitivity issues Students may need training in asking clarifying questions and providing supportive remarks Teacher might want to broadly define specific areas to prevent limiting students' thinking Provide example; ask students for another example to clarify possible misinterpretations Sharing with another student might be ill advised if students are unfamiliar or sensitive about receiving feedback

Rating Yourself

Directions: Circle the number for each item that best describes you.

	Strength	Good	Average	Not So Hot	Weakness
Social Self					
Making new friends	1	2	3	4	5
Being a good friend	1	2	3	4	5
Inviting friends	1	2	3	4	5
Listening	1	2	3	4	5
Starting conversations	1	2	3	4	5
Keeping conversations going	1	2	3	4	5
Sharing resources	1	2	3	4	5
Getting over arguments	1	2	3	4	5
Helping friends	1	2	3	4	5
Being popular	1	2	3	4	5
Being a leader	1	2	3	4	5
Working with others	1	2	3	4	5
Physical Self					
Grooming	1	2	3	4	5
Sports	1	2	3	4	5
Health	1	2	3	4	5
Nutrition	1	2	3	4	5
Exercise	1	2	3	4	5
Appearance	1	2	3	4	5
Creative Self					
Art	1	2	3	4	5
Music	1	2	3	4	5
Drama	1	2	3	4	5
Writing/poetry	1	2	3	4	5
Building things	1	2	3	4	5
Other _____	1	2	3	4	5
Spiritual/Moral Self					
Thinking about, deciding what you believe	1	2	3	4	5
Learning about other people's beliefs	1	2	3	4	5
Helping others	1	2	3	4	5
Following rules	1	2	3	4	5

Check for Understanding Self-Awareness

Success Attribute Covered	Self-Awareness
Familiarity with Success Attributes	Intermediate lesson Follow up to initial discussion of self-awareness and related concepts
Suggested Grade Level	Grades 3 to 12
Objective(s)	To define and understand self-awareness
Materials Needed	Worksheet for each group Poster paper or boards Markers Scissors Wide variety of magazines	Selection of stories or videos about individuals with disabilities (see Appendix A for suggested media)
Approximate Time	1 hour Additional time may be needed to read books, watch videos

Directions to Implement the Activity	Explain that this is a follow-up activity to the discussion of self-awareness
	
	Students will assemble a collage as a group:
	
	    Collage will represent group's ideas about the strengths and weaknesses of a real or fictitious person (key character)
	
	Review key self-awareness terms
	
	Review rules for working cooperatively
	
	Assign students to groups
	
	As whole class or in small groups, students will read or watch a video about a real or fictitious person with a disability or other challenge who was successful (referred to as the *key character*)
	
	Ask students to answer questions on worksheets about that key person:
	
	    Encourage creating ideas based on evidence from the story
	
	When worksheets are complete, explain how to assemble a collage:
	
	    Select pictures that represent idea
	    Have enough pictures to fill the page; overlapping is allowed; little or no empty space should be left
	    Remove pictures from magazines by cutting or ripping
	    Remind students about sharing magazines and other supplies
	    Have designated procedures for taking and returning supplies
	    Establish limits of talking and sharing among students

	Assign students a role assembling the collage or finding, cutting, or gluing pictures
	Monitor group's progress assembling the collage
	When complete, students may explain their creation, relating it to the key character
Suggested Modifications	Assign roles for each student in group, based on strengths (ability to find good pictures quickly, ability to tear out or cut usable pictures, ability to add words or drawings as needed)
	May want to have precut pictures available ahead of time
Caveats Regarding Possible Sensitivity of Topic	Some students may be unfamiliar with their disabilities
	Other students may disclose information about themselves that cause others to question them
	Moderating comments or asking students to record a question or thought for later may be necessary

Check for Understanding Self-Awareness

Directions: Answer each of the questions in your own words.

Self-awareness is:

_____

_____

1. What were the key character's strengths?

_____

_____

2. What were the key character's weaknesses?

_____

_____

3. How might the key character's strengths have helped make him or her important?

_____

_____

4. How did the key character's weaknesses help make him or her important?

_____

_____

Describing Self

Success Attribute Covered	Self-Awareness
Familiarity with Success Attributes	Intermediate lesson
Suggested Grade Level	Grades 1 to 12
Objective(s)	To gain awareness of feelings, opinions, and personal values and how they relate to those of other individuals
Materials Needed	Worksheet for each student Various magazines that can be cut Glue, glue sticks, tape Scissors or rulers to help remove pictures from magazines Markers
Approximate Time	1 hour
Directions to Implement the Activity	Indicate that the class will begin exploring ways to describe themselves to other people for the following reasons: Get to know each other better so the students can help each other May use ideas if meeting someone for the first time May be interviewed for a job Get to know each other so class is a more comfortable place for learning Explain procedures to make a collage: Select pictures that represent idea Have enough pictures to fill the page; overlapping is allowed; little or no empty space left Remove pictures from magazines by cutting or ripping Remind students about sharing magazines and other supplies Have designated procedures for taking and returning supplies Establish limits of talking and sharing among students Monitor students as they find pictures and assemble collages: Remind them of the time allowance After responding to the question at the bottom of the worksheet, students should explain their collage to either the entire class or a small group of other students All collages should be displayed in the room for a time and then saved for follow-up in several weeks As self-awareness activities continue, students may refer to the first collages to determine their changes and growth over the year

Suggested Modifications	Assist student with finding graphics by questioning the individual about interests, likes
	Present one or two pictures at a time to the student to seek clarification about individual wants
	May ask other students to formulate questions to help student assemble a list of possible pictures
	Either assign small groups or pairs to work together, or allow conversation and sharing of ideas as the project happens
	As pictures are selected, ask student to explain the selections
	Before student presents collage to the class, rehearse the presentation by selecting or grouping pictures for the discussion
	As a follow-up activity, students may be asked to write an essay explaining the meaning of their collage
Caveats Regarding Possible Sensitivity of Topic	Have wide selection of magazines and pictures available so students' reports are not skewed by limited graphics
	Monitor students as they select pictures
	Query students' selections to determine the possibility of disclosure issues. Students may make sensitive personal information public. Other group members may have difficulty accepting that information, so the teacher may need to discuss acceptance with all students /or monitor behavior that might occur later.
	Ensure that students are willing to share their collage to small groups or the entire class
	Check that students understand collages will be displayed

Describing Self

Directions: Create your collage here.

_____

(title)

[ ]

How does your collage describe you?_____

_____

_____

_____

Describing Likes and Dislikes

Success Attribute Covered	Self-Awareness
Familiarity with Success Attributes	Beginning
Suggested Grade Level	Grades 1 to 12
Objective(s)	To develop awareness of strengths, weaknesses, and talents in various contexts
Materials Needed	Worksheet for each student Pens and pencils Materials to make or display a graph
Approximate Time	45 minutes
Directions to Implement the Activity	Follow-up to the previous collage exercise to gain further knowledge of themselves Explain that many times strengths are something a person likes to do, and weaknesses are something a person dislikes Distribute worksheets, pens and pencils, rulers (for tracking) Direct students to complete worksheets, independently giving each student an ID number so data can be collected anonymously Collect worksheets and either immediately or at a later time have students (some or all) assemble the data in a bar graph or some other graphic presentation Discuss findings as a group or ask students to write a small conclusion
Suggested Modifications	Assist student by reading individual items Clarify that students understand the concepts of likes and dislikes
Caveats Regarding Possible Sensitivity of Topic	Student answer may be significantly different and known to group, so monitor for possible bullying. If a student's answer might be viewed as odd or abnormal or uncool by the other members of the group, monitor the students for possible bullying.

Describing Likes and Dislikes

Directions: How good are you at each of the following things? Put a check under either **Likes** or **Dislikes**.

At School	Likes	Dislikes
Reading	_____	_____
Math	_____	_____
Listening to directions	_____	_____
Asking for help	_____	_____
Art	_____	_____
Playing with friends	_____	_____
Games	_____	_____
Sports	_____	_____
At Home		
Chores (taking care of pets, making bed)	_____	_____
Listening to parents	_____	_____
Doing homework	_____	_____
Playing with friends	_____	_____
Playing with brothers or sisters	_____	_____

Compare and Contrast Success Attributes

Success Attribute Covered	Self-Awareness, Proactivity, Perseverance
Familiarity with Success Attributes	Intermediate lesson Completed after students have been introduced to at least the three success attributes of self-awareness, proactivity, and perseverance Students must have some knowledge; may serve as an assessment of how much knowledge they have gained at the point
Suggested Grade Level	Grades 4 to 12
Objective(s)	To define and differentiate among the success attributes
Materials Needed	Worksheet for each group of no more than four students Large sheets of paper Glue Markers Variety of magazines with pictures
Approximate Time	1 hour

Directions to Implement the Activity	Explain that this is a check of the students' knowledge of some of the success attributes
	
	Assign one of the three success attributes to each group
	
	Explain that they will develop a collage based on that attribute and its synonyms
	
	Encourage each group to give pictures to other groups that work for them (for instance, a member of the perseverance groups finds a picture that will work for the proactivity group)
	
	Group work rules should be reviewed:
	
	    Words and drawings are allowed
	    Respect others' contributions
	    Pictures can be cut or torn
	    Division of tasks is clear (who and when will cut, tear, glue, and so forth)
	
	Posters are made while the teacher observes, questions
	
	When posters are completed and the room is clean, each group explains their poster

Suggested Modifications	Check magazines for appropriateness and enough variety
Caveats Regarding Possible Sensitivity of Topic	Assign students who are supportive of one another's contributions May want to assign based on understanding of a particular attribute

Compare and Contrast Success Attributes

Names of group members:

_____

_____

Our Success Attribute: _____

Dictionary definition of our Success Attribute:

_____

_____

Definition of our Success Attribute in our group's words:

_____

_____

Synonyms for our Success Attribute:

_____   _____

_____   _____

_____   _____

I See Me, You See Me

Success Attribute Covered	Self-Awareness
Familiarity with Success Attributes	Introductory lesson
Suggested Grade Level	Grades 1 to 12
Objective(s)	To develop awareness of others' views
Materials Needed	Worksheet for each student Overhead of worksheet Pens and pencils
Approximate Time	60 minutes (may split activity over four or five days)
Directions to Implement the Activity	Brainstorm with class to list people's strengths, emphasizing how varied the strengths might be (social, physical, emotional, social, academic, problem solving) Ask that students think about their own strengths, and have students list those under the question on the worksheet Hypothesize how others might see them, and have students list those under the question Ask for volunteers to share, and, if appropriate, ask students for their reasoning behind their choices Ask students to describe what they learned from this exercise
Suggested Modifications	Draw pictures or icons to represent characteristics as a substitute for writing If students have difficulty hypothesizing how other see them, suggest possible people (parents, grandparents); may need to provide circumstance ("When you get a good grade, how do your parents see you?")
Caveats Regarding Possible Sensitivity of Topic	Monitor closely for students' reactions to others' reports of themselves May need to monitor during transition or free time for possible bullying or others' attention to individual student's characteristics Emphasize classroom rules about acceptance, listening, and support

Name: _____   Date: _____

I See Me, You See Me

How do you see your strengths?

_____

_____

How do you think others see your strengths?

_____

_____

What did you learn?

_____

_____

_____

_____

Check Out Sparktop.org

Success Attribute Covered	Self-Awareness, Emotional Coping Strategies
Familiarity with Success Attributes	Introductory lesson
Suggested Grade Level	Grades 5 to 10
Objective(s)	To develop an understanding of learning disabilities
Materials Needed	Worksheet for each student
	Computer with Internet access
	Pencils
	Optional: projection system for teacher explanation and modeling
Approximate Time	50 minutes
Directions to Implement the Activity	Explain to students that they will be examining a Web site designed for them that will allow them to explore ideas related to learning disabilities:
	Much of the Web site contains contributions from students their age
	Explain that the purpose of this exercise is to familiarize them with the components of the Web site
	Once students have completed their individual explorations, they may want to discuss their likes and dislikes, possible future uses
Suggested Modifications	Headphones while using the computer will allow minimal distraction
	Younger students may be paired with slightly older students so that the worksheet might be completed as a team
	Might use older students who are familiar with the Web site to demonstrate parts to students who might struggle with distractibility
	If projection system is available, initially modeling how to navigate parts of the site might be helpful to some students
Caveats Regarding Possible Sensitivity of Topic	The Web site addresses students using the terms *learning disabilities* and *ADD/ADHD*, which may need further teacher explanation or elaboration
	If students struggle with their challenges or are not diagnosed, the Web site might be helpful, but some discussion prior to using it might make it more student-friendly

Check Out Sparktop.org

Directions: Go to the Internet, type in www.sparktop.org, and log on as a GUEST.

This is a site for kids (and teens) with learning disabilities or attention problems, or both. There is information about learning disabilities (LD), Attention Deficit Disorder (ADD), and Hyperactivity (ADHD). It has lots to do—for example:

Games to play

Teen mentors to ask questions of

Art projects to try

Hints about coping with LD

Getting organized

Famous people with LD

E-mail pen pals to hook up with

What I liked in EXPLORE:

_____

_____

What I tried in CREATE:

_____

_____

What I played in GAMES:

_____

_____

How I used CONNECT:

_____

_____

I RECOMMEND trying on Sparktop.org:

_____

_____

Here is what I learned about my strengths and weaknesses:

_____

_____

_____

_____

Identify Favorite Activities

Success Attribute Covered	Self-Awareness
Familiarity with Success Attributes	Intermediate lesson
Suggested Grade Level	Grades 1 to 12
Objective(s)	To recognize and accept talents along with limitations
Materials Needed	Worksheet for each student Pens and pencils Overhead of worksheet for teacher's explanations
Approximate Time	45 minutes
Directions to Implement the Activity	Review of concepts related to self-awareness Focus on strengths; one way to identify strengths is to examine activities during and after school. If students can state their activity preference or report excitement about participating in an activity or if they can give rationales about why they like an activity, they may be developing ways to find their strengths. Reinforce the importance of personal preference and accepting others' responses that might disagree May (or not) share responses with small group or entire class Check responses for clarity, readable spelling Put completed worksheets with other self-awareness activities; will be referenced in later exercises
Suggested Modifications	Students may need to be paired with a peer or an adult for reading and recording answers May need to prompt or encourage students to complete worksheet May need to discuss what *favorite* means (use food, music as examples for student to clarify concept) May need to develop a list of choices; however, that may limit students' responses
Caveats Regarding Possible Sensitivity of Topic	Monitor students' responses for possible quirky answers that might generate a negative response from other students Reinforce students who make supportive comments or ask questions of others

Identify Favorite Activities

1. When you have free time at home, what do you do?

   Favorites

   _____

   Next favorites

   _____

   Next favorites

   _____

2. When you have free time at school, what do you do?

   Favorites

   _____

   Next favorites

   _____

   Next favorites

   _____

3. After-school activities you are in: (sports, music, art class, dance, scouts)

   _____

4. Favorite subjects in school:

   _____

5. Do you have hobbies? List them here:

   _____

   _____

6. If a teacher asked you to do a project, what would you choose to do?

   _____

Freaky Friday

Success Attribute Covered	Self-Awareness, Goal Setting, Perseverance, Social Support Systems
Familiarity with Success Attributes	Intermediate lesson
Suggested Grade Level	Grades 3 to 12
Objective(s)	To set realistic goals
	To develop an awareness of coping strategies to compensate for learning disabilities
Materials Needed	Worksheet for each student
	Pens and pencils
	Magazines
Approximate Time	30 minutes
Directions to Implement the Activity	May want or need to show the movie or read the book *Freaky Friday* or set the scenario (child-parent trade bodies and have to live each other's lives for a time)
	Discuss what the students might do if they had to do a family member's job for a day
	Discuss what skills might be needed for a variety of jobs
	Review the terms *strengths*, *weaknesses*, and *interests*
	Examine and explain the parts of the worksheets that students should do independently
	Monitor students as they answer individual questions
	As a whole group, select a volunteer for one or two answers
Suggested Modifications	If students have limited familiarity with skills needed for a particular job, may do a preliminary assignment as homework:
	Ask students to interview several family members (extended family too) to find out one or more of the jobs they have had in their lives and the skills needed for each one
	Students could reference that information in the beginning stages of the discussion in class
	Have students work in pairs to complete the worksheet, or allow students to ask one another for assistance
	For students who complete their work earlier than the rest, ask them to find pictures in magazines that represent the jobs discussed in class for discussions in the future

Caveats Regarding Possible Sensitivity of Topic	May need to modify for specific family situations by having students select a family member's job
	Students may begin to come to some realization about the realism of career choice during this assignment, which may result in a need for an individual discussion with an adult
	Students may need to be reminded that life choices change and that nothing is final, so taking a risk in this assignment should be supported by others
	Students may be sensitive about a parent's job choice and may elect to discuss or use someone else during the discussion

Name: _____   Date: _____

Freaky Friday

Everything has changed! Now everyone has to get a job, INCLUDING KIDS AND TEENAGERS! Write your interests and talents. Then write down the job you *could* do, given what you know and can do TODAY!

My Interests   My Talents

_____

_____   _____

_____   _____

_____

One job I think I *could* do today:

_____

How I think my interests and talents match the job I chose:

_____

_____

I Feel Good About Me

Success Attribute Covered	Self-Awareness
Familiarity with Success Attributes	Advanced lesson
Suggested Grade Level	Grades 1 to 12
Objective(s)	To enhance general self-acceptance as well as acceptance of learning disability
Materials Needed	Worksheet for each student Highlighters Notebook of completed worksheets Sticky notes
Approximate Time	2 hours (may want to break into two sessions)

Directions to Implement the Activity	Explain purpose of this work: sometimes it is necessary to explain your strengths and weaknesses to a person you might not know well or have just met (employers, teachers):
	
	  Students need to know how to express this message clearly and briefly
	
	  Sometimes a student might need to quickly state a strength or weakness without adding extra data (if the task does not require the student to read, describing struggles with reading is not necessary)
	
	  Students need confidence understanding that if they express a concern about a weakness, they should conversely be able to state a related strength: "I don't read well, but I work hard, persevere, and problem-solve well."
	
	Distribute completed worksheets, notes, and materials from other classes to each student (if needed)
	
	Ask students to review their previous work and highlight information that is common throughout or seems key to the assignment sheet
	
	Explain that students should complete one to three of the worksheet sections as they relate to their personal strengths
	
	After checking for accuracy and completeness, students should practice delivering their information about strengths and weaknesses to two or three other students (and teacher, if needed) before presenting their reports to the whole class

Suggested Modifications	Review information to go into the blanks Revise information as needed to address students' strengths Some of the statements on the worksheets may need to be modified to fit specific individuals

Caveats Regarding Possible Sensitivity of Topic	May be difficult for some students to express their areas of strength:
	May need individual encouragement to express to another person Repeated practice with known supportive individuals may be necessary
	May be equally difficult for some students to identify their weaknesses

I Feel Good About Me

Directions: Fill in the blanks with answers that best describe who you are.

Physical

My best sport is _____, because I'm _____

I _____ for my health all the time.

I think my _____ looks about right.

My best physical feature is _____

One silly thing I can do with my body is _____

I struggle with _____

Creative

The last thing I did that was creative was _____

I like to _____

I am good at _____

I need encouragement to _____

Social

I know I am a good friend when I _____

The best thing about being my friend is _____

I help others by _____

To make other people laugh, I _____

To get over arguments, I _____

I need help to _____

Students who are proactive:

- Are actively engaged in the world around them
- Tend to socialize
- Participate in community activities
- Take an active role in their families, neighborhoods, and friendship groups
- Believe they have the power to control their own destiny and affect the outcome of their lives
- Are able to make decisions and act on those decisions to control their lives
- Consult with others while making decisions
- Are flexible in considering and weighing options
- Take responsibility for both the positive and negative outcomes of their decisions

Introduction to Proactivity

Success Attribute Covered	Proactivity
Familiarity with Success Attributes	Introductory lesson
Suggested Grade Level	Grades 3 to 12
Objective(s)	To define proactivity and identify concepts related to it
Materials Needed	Worksheet for each student Pens and pencils Chalkboard or display board for teacher notes
Approximate Time	50 minutes

Directions to Implement the Activity	Explain the importance of proactivity to success (see the Introduction to this book)
	
	Define *proactivity*, and relate the following terms to proactivity; as concepts are discussed, ask students to takes notes on these facets:
	
	    Making good decisions
	    Integrity
	    Self-control; take charge of self
	    Networking
	    Personal responsibility (including eating good food, sleeping well, keeping body healthy)
	    Being a good student
	    Actively participating in:
	
	        Community
	        School
	        Place of worship
	        Family
	
	    Engaging in world
	
	        Economically
	        Politically
	        Socially
	
	Ask students to identify examples that demonstrate their understanding of the terms

Suggested Modifications	Select the number of terms used based on the students' comprehension Help students take notes; have note takers available Encourage verbalizing for questions, clarification
Caveats Regarding Possible Sensitivity of Topic	Students may be able to comprehend proactivity but have difficulty applying it to their own lives May need multiple experiences with practice; embed into vocabulary and academic areas where possible

Name: _____   Date: _____

Introduction to Proactivity

Directions: Follow the teacher's directions and fill in the spaces below.

1. Write one sentence to define *proactivity:*

   _____

2. Write the definition of the following terms in your own words:

   a. *Making good decisions* _____

   _____

   b. *Integrity* _____

   _____

   c. *Self-control; take charge of self* _____

   _____

   d. *Networking* _____

   _____

   e. *Personal responsibility* (including eating good food, sleeping well, keeping healthy) __

   _____

   f. *Being a good student* _____

   _____

   g. *Actively participating in:*

   Community _____

   _____

   School _____

   _____

   Place of worship _____

   _____

Family _____

_____

h. *Engaging in the world:*

Economically _____

_____

Politically _____

_____

Socially _____

_____

3. Write one sentence about how you are proactive, using at least one of the terms you discussed in class:

_____

_____

Finding Help

Success Attribute Covered	Proactivity
Familiarity with Success Attributes	Intermediate lesson
Suggested Grade Level	Grades 1 to 12
Objective(s)	To develop strategies for engaging in the world
Materials Needed	Worksheet for each student Pens and pencils Chalkboard
Approximate Time	30 minutes
Directions to Implement the Activity	Review concepts and vocabulary related to proactivity Explain worksheet to class; ask students to write the first answer that comes to mind for each questions When students finish, ask for volunteers for answers, collecting multiple responses for each item Compile the various answers, and note why each may be correct When responses have been listed for each question, emphasize the importance of knowing more than one resource in the community (or the student's surroundings)
Suggested Modifications	Reduce the number of questions; ask different questions over several days Have a sense of the resources within the community that students may use; ask family members for additional information about out-of-school resources
Caveats Regarding Possible Sensitivity of Topic	Be aware of possible sensitivity students have based on economic or social differences within a class

Finding Help

Directions: Write the first answer that comes to mind to each question on the line provided.

1. Whom do you ask when you:

   a. need help with homework? _____

   b. cannot reach something on a shelf? _____

   c. are locked out of your house? _____

   d. left your lunch at home? _____

   e. lose something important? _____

2. Where do you go when you:

   a. want an after-school exercise class? _____

   b. want a book to read? _____

   c. need directions to a store? _____

   d. need to have a computer repaired? _____

   e. are hungry? _____

The Six Success Factors for Children with Learning Disabilities

Unlock Closed Doors

Success Attribute Covered	Proactivity
Familiarity with Success Attributes	Intermediate lesson
Suggested Grade Level	Grades 1 to 12
Objective(s)	To take an active role in their families, neighborhoods, and friendship groups
Materials Needed	Movie or book from resource list in Appendix A under proactivity (or another media selection with focus on proactivity)
	Worksheet for each student
	Pens and pencils
Approximate Time	Time to read or view media
Directions to Implement the Activity	Review the concepts and terms related to proactivity
	Explain that students can learn by observing others who demonstrate proactivity
	Introduce the media selection, and assign students to read, watch, or listen (as appropriate); may be appropriate to do as a class, in small groups, or independently
	Upon completion of the story, ask students to respond to the worksheet questions
	Ask students to share their responses and lead the class in a discussion of a common definition of proactivity
Suggested Modifications	Assist students with writing
	Check for understanding of terms related to proactivity
	Keep the list of terms and concepts posted while students are responding to the questions
Caveats Regarding Possible Sensitivity of Topic	Select materials that best match needs of student

Unlock Closed Doors

Directions: After finishing the story, answer the questions in your own words.

Title of book or movie: _____

1. Describe the main character.

   _____

   _____

2. List some reasons that the main character was not proactive at the beginning of the story.

   _____

   _____

3. List some reasons that you think the main character was proactive at the end of the story.

   _____

   _____

4. In your opinion, what were obstacles that prevented the main character from being proactive?

   _____

   _____

5. What would you have done if you were the main character?

   _____

   _____

Ask the Experts

Success Attribute Covered	**Proactivity**
Familiarity with Success Attributes	Intermediate lesson
Suggested Grade Level	Grades 1 to 12
Objective(s)	To develop self-confidence to ask questions of others
Materials Needed	Worksheet for each student Pens and pencils Materials and supplies for experts to use

Approximate Time	Two separate class periods:
	
	    First day for establishing expertise
	    Second day for demonstrations

Directions to Implement the Activity	Review (or introduce) seeking out an expert when we have a question or need a problem solved as a part of proactivity
	
	Ask the class to define *expert*, and list some related concepts, examples
	
	Insist that each member of the class is an expert at something:
	
	    Teacher should use himself or herself as a model
	
	After teacher models how to completes a copy of the worksheet, students fill in their responses
	
	On second day, teacher displays each student's expertise
	
	Rotating through the class, small groups of students with a designated time limit will be assigned to an area of the room to demonstrate their expertise
	
	Other members of class should be assigned to groups to rotate through the stations to meet with the expert and ask questions or see demonstration
	
	Monitor groups to assist with supporting both experts and audience
	
	As follow-up, students should provide feedback about both experiences:
	
	    If possible, students write about both experiences as a follow-up assignment

Suggested Modifications	Teacher may identify specific areas for students' expertise (perhaps initially considering academics, visual arts, physical education):
	May need to ask family members for input about an area of expertise
	Student may need instruction about providing audience support to the expert during presentations
	An additional class period for instruction on asking questions, giving supportive feedback, and so on
Caveats Regarding Possible Sensitivity of Topic	Students may feel too much pressure to teach expertise (an alternative may be to have a display board or PowerPoint presentation that will show their expertise and lessen their immediate involvement
	Students may feel that they have no expertise, so knowing students well to guide them to an area may be necessary

Ask the Experts

I'm an Expert

Directions: Fill in the blanks.

I am an expert in: _____

I have been an expert for: _____

I became an expert by:

_____

_____

Three facts about my expertise are:

1. _____

2. _____

3. _____

Ask an Expert

Expert's Name: _____

Expertise: _____

I learned these three things from this expert:

1. _____

2. _____

3. _____

Take Action

Success Attribute Covered	Proactivity, Emotional Coping
Familiarity with Success Attributes	Introductory lesson
Suggested Grade Level	Grades 3 to 12
Objective(s)	To make decisions and act on those decisions while understanding the advantages and disadvantages of making a choice
Materials Needed	Worksheet for each student Pens and pencils Overheads of worksheets and additional scenarios (or both)
Approximate Time	50 minutes
Directions to Implement the Activities	Introduce the concepts related to proactivity for this assignment: Proactive (making a plan, talking to a friend, asking an adult, working toward a solution) Passive (doing nothing, ignoring, doing something unrelated and unhelpful) List possible advantages to being proactive (get what you want, feel in control, don't feel helpless, people respect your opinion) and disadvantages (might be physically dangerous, could lead to severe consequences, lose a friend who sees you as too bossy) Individuals or groups respond to the six scenarios listed on the worksheet Ask for volunteers to share responses Ask students to complete questions 7 through 10 independently or in assigned small groups Volunteers should share one of their answers from the second page Use the student reports to review the concept of proactivity Collect and save the students' scenarios for future classes
Suggested Modifications	Collect a file of possible scenarios to use when introducing proactivity Modify the scenarios provided to fit a particular setting May pair students to complete one worksheet per pair Discuss in small groups, with one person recording conclusions

The Six Success Factors for Children with Learning Disabilities

Select two or three of the scenarios, and hold a class discussion (make sure that each student had the opportunity to share ideas during the discussion by using a checklist of student names)

With scenario modifications (perhaps adding examples from work settings), would be appropriate for older students

Caveats Regarding Possible Sensitivity of Topic	Carefully create scenarios that address realistic problems without pinpointing a specific student

Take Action!

Directions: Read each statement below, and write two possible actions a person might take. One of the actions should be *proactive* (making a plan, talking to a friend, asking an adult, working toward a solution), and one should be *passive* (doing nothing, ignoring, doing something unrelated and unhelpful). Decide if your action is safe by writing *yes* or *no* in the space provided.

1. Your assignment is too hard.

    Passive: _____   Is it safe? _____

    Proactive: _____   Is it safe? _____

2. Someone on the ball court takes the ball away from you.

    Passive: _____   Is it safe? _____

    Proactive: _____   Is it safe? _____

3. You want to make friends with a certain person.

    Passive: _____   Is it safe ?_____

    Proactive: _____   Is it safe? _____

4. You rip your shirt on the field and are embarrassed to wear it to the next class.

    Passive:_____   Is it safe? _____

    Proactive: _____   Is it safe? _____

5. You lose your backpack.

    Passive: _____   Is it safe? _____

    Proactive: _____   Is it safe? _____

6. Your two best friends get into a fistfight.

    Passive: _____   Is it safe? _____

    Proactive: _____   Is it safe? _____

7. Describe a problem you had where you were passive.

_____

_____

8. Was there a better action for the above problem?

_____

_____

9. Describe a problem you had where you were proactive.

_____

_____

10. Was there a better action for this problem?

_____

_____

11. List one possible time next week when you will practice being proactive.

_____

Make the Solution Work for You

Success Attribute Covered	Proactivity
Familiarity with Success Attributes	Advanced lesson
Suggested Grade Level	Grades 3 to 12
Objective(s)	To be flexible in considering and weighing options
Materials Needed	A worksheet for each student
	Examples of problems (magazine and newspaper articles, news clips, videos of fiction)
Approximate Time	50 minutes
Directions to Implement the Activity	Define *proactivity* using terms, descriptions from the Introduction to book, emphasizing those related to examples
	Highlight the idea that being proactive involves the ability to define the problem and generate possible solutions
	Present an event:
	If there is a current problem in school, use that
	If not, an event from the news or a short story can be used
	The event should be brief, have a readily identifiable problem, and need a couple of solutions—for instance:
	Students disrupting classes as they move to other classes
	Students forgetting lunches at home
	People talking on cell phones in movie theaters
	Using the worksheet questions, model one or two events for the class
	Present the class with one or several events, and ask them to complete the worksheet either independently or in pairs
	Discuss the variety of responses
	Review the terms related to proactivity relative to the solutions generated
Suggested Modifications	Complete the worksheet as a class
	Ask students to generate possible events from their lives
Caveats Regarding Possible Sensitivity of Topic	During individual or group work, make sure the students stay focused
	Selected events may cause unexpected reactions with students, so prepare for possible follow-up with individual students

The Six Success Factors for Children with Learning Disabilities

Make the Solution Work for You

Directions: Using either the teacher's example of a problem or creating one, write the answers to the questions below.

1. What is the problem?

   _____

   _____

2. What are some solutions?

   _____

   _____

3. For each solution:

   Is it safe? _____

   How will it make people feel? _____

   Is it fair? _____

   Will it work? _____

4. Choose a solution and use it:

   Did it work?

   _____

   _____

5. Is there something else that needs to be done? What might happen if you tried another solution?

   _____

   _____

How Most People Find Jobs

Success Attribute Covered	Proactivity
Familiarity with Success Attributes	Introductory lesson
Suggested Grade Level	Grades 1 to 12
Objective(s)	To consult others while making decisions
Materials Needed	Worksheet for each student Pens and pencils
Approximate Time	30 minutes class time plus homework or out-of-class time
Directions to Implement the Activity	This may be used as a follow-up to a career exploration unit Discuss the importance of proactivity to finding a job: Ask students to brainstorm possibilities, related concepts Distribute worksheet, and explain each of the terms and how to complete the assignment, noting that instructions are on worksheet Check that students understand how much time this assignment needs for completion Highlight due dates and consequences for timely submissions Graph the group responses, and formulate summary statements about results
Suggested Modifications	Limit the interviews to one or two people Have students use audio recorders to limit writing, or have student ask adult to write response on appropriate line May need to contact the family to discuss assignment Assignment may need to be completed in school with support personnel acting as interviewees
Caveats Regarding Possible Sensitivity of Topic	Students who are capable of completing the assignment on their own but do not submit work Students who have limited access to working adults

How Most People Find Jobs

Directions: Interview FIVE adults who are now working, and ask each one this question: "How did you get your job?" Then write down the names after each response they give you.

Through a close friend or family member:

_____

_____

Through a neighbor or acquaintance from a social group: (for example, sports team, yoga class, church)

_____

_____

From a newspaper:

_____

_____

Through a personal contact from previous job:

_____

_____

Recruited by a rival employer:

_____

_____

Through a contact from a professional organization you belong to:

_____

_____

Other:

_____

_____

Am I Ready to Be On My Own?

Success Attribute Covered	Proactivity, Self-Awareness, Social Support Systems
Familiarity with Success Attributes	Introductory lesson
Suggested Grade Level	Grades 3 to 12
Objective(s)	To practice making decisions about controlling one's own life
Materials Needed	Worksheet for each student Pencils Rulers for tracking responses for each student
Approximate Time	50 minutes
Directions to Implement the Activity	Briefly discuss the challenges of living on one's own Explain that this is a little check to assess readiness Distribute and explain worksheets Individually, students should put a check in the first column for skills they are able to complete independently now They should put a check in the second column if they think they will need the skill in the future In the final column, students should predict at what age they will master the skill When all students are finished, ask for their responses by item: Perhaps determine which skills most students have now or which skills students anticipate needing, be willing to learn (even if it sounded unpleasant or uninteresting); other skills may be added to sheet as needed Give class feedback as a whole; may want to present as bar graph Conduct further discussions about responses that seem out of the ordinary or confusing
Suggested Modifications	Assistance with reading, tracking skills Clarification of specific terms For students who finish quickly, ask them to begin developing a list of what they will need specifically to achieve one of the skills they identified as willing to learn Results may lead to follow-up lessons regarding the skills or their prerequisites
Caveats Regarding Possible Sensitivity of Topic	If a student may be unable to perform a particular skill (motor skills may prohibit some tasks), discuss with that individual beforehand. That student may want to relay his or her strategies for achieving independence (using greater support services) or may wish to explain the dangers of doing specific tasks independently while addressing his or her strengths: "I'm not able to do this task, but I can do that task well."

The Six Success Factors for Children with Learning Disabilities

Name: _____ Date: _____

Am I Ready to Be On My Own?

Directions: Answer the first two questions at the top by putting a check on the line by the skill listed. If you check the second question, answer the third question by putting the age you will be when you can do the skill.

I Can Do This Now	I Will Need to Be Able to Do This in the Future	How Old I Will Be When I Can Do This
Finances		
Write a check	_____	_____
Balance my checkbook	_____	_____
Figure out how much money I need per month	_____	_____
Pay my share of expenses	_____	_____
Do online banking	_____	_____
Chores		
Pick up my stuff	_____	_____
Do dishes	_____	_____
Take out garbage	_____	_____
Share chores	_____	_____
Clothing/Grooming		
Do laundry	_____	_____
Budget for clothes	_____	_____
Budget for grooming products	_____	_____
Get a haircut	_____	_____
Iron my clothes	_____	_____
Transportation		
Know how to use public transportation	_____	_____
Know how to drive	_____	_____
Know the costs (gas, insurance, repairs, bus fare)	_____	_____

Food

Grocery shop   _____   _____

Know what my body needs   _____   _____

Cook a meal   _____   _____

Clean up   _____   _____

Emergencies

Call 911   _____   _____

Call someone if stranded   _____   _____

Find health center, doctor, hospital, dentist   _____   _____

Call home   _____   _____

Roommates

Choose one   _____   _____

Get along   _____   _____

Share with him or her   _____   _____

Give "space"   _____   _____

Change my annoying habits   _____   _____

Share expenses   _____   _____

Discuss having guests   _____   _____

Make and stick to agreements   _____   _____

_____   _____   _____

_____   _____   _____

What Do I Know? What Must I Learn?

Success Attribute Covered	**Proactivity, Self-Awareness, Perseverance, Goal Setting**
Familiarity with Success Attributes	Although the worksheet can be done without any knowledge of the Success Attributes, in-depth discussion about the attributes based on the students' findings requires advance familiarity with all of the Success Attributes
Suggested Grade Level	Grades 7 to 12
Objective(s)	To gain awareness of the skills needed to survive and succeed as an independent adult
Materials Needed	Worksheet for each student Pencils Rulers for tracking items
Approximate Time	50 minutes
Directions to Implement the Activity	Discuss the importance of considering multiple (and sometimes unrelated) tasks as an adult; focus on using the Success Attributes of proactivity, self-awareness, perseverance, and goal setting to assist a person with completing groups of tasks successfully
	Distribute the worksheet, and explain that it should be treated seriously; students' answers will vary
	Students will need to mark the survey with one of four abbreviations; perhaps an efficient way is to first mark the tasks students already know, then review the lists and mark the tasks they will need to know next year, followed by a list review marking what needs to be known when they are eighteen years old, and then a final review indicating what needs to be done by the time they are ready to start a family
	Allow a brief amount of time to add to the list as needed
	The group might want to decide which of the tasks require help, need practice, take time to master
	In assigned small groups, students should share some or all of their responses
	Discuss putting tasks into categories; either most important or immediate, or within areas like hygiene, medical, transportation, work

	May wish to provide follow-up activities to identify individual strengths and weaknesses based on findings:
	
	    Set one or two short- or long-term goals to address personal concerns
	    Discuss as a group how perseverance is required for student-selected items

Suggested Modifications	Students may need help reading or defining specific tasks
	Highlight one cluster of items, and ask students to respond to clusters over several days
Caveats Regarding Possible Sensitivity of Topic	Students may be unwilling to share their results with the class
	May want to make broad categories, complete time line with the specific tasks during class, and then conference individually with students to address tasks that they may need to practice immediately

What Do I Know? What Must I Learn?

Directions: For each one of the items, write one of the following four abbreviations just before it:

AK	Things I already know
NY	Things I'll need to know how to do next year
18	Things I will need to know how to do by age 18
SF	Things I will need to know how to do before I start a family

cook my own meals	buy furniture	decide on a college
wash dishes	drive a car	read traffic signs
buy my own groceries	parallel-park a car	ride a bicycle
get a haircut	take the bus/ metro	swim
brush my teeth	buy a house	play common board game
shave	pass a driver's test	plant a tree
choose outfits to wear	make a doctor's appointment	mow the lawn
dress myself	get an ambulance	use a power saw
do laundry	eat nutritiously	replace a light bulb
buy a car	get a promotion	clean the bathroom
buy a house	get a raise	vacuum
balance my checkbook	baby sit for 4 hours	buy furniture to fit room
get credit card	answer the telephone	visit parents
get credit to buy something	find my way when lost	get a mortgage
take medication as directed	make a budget	write a check
rent an apartment	write a résumé	baby sit for 24 hours
read a utility bill	apply for a job	care for a baby 24/7
read the newspaper	do well in an interview	pass a college essay
read a want ad	make friends	pass a college course

get accommodations at college

send out résumés

ask for or agree to go on a date

choose clothes for job interview

say no to drugs

write cover letters

get accommodations on the job

report a crime

apply to colleges

avoid an accident

sign my name

traffic accident

put out a fire

check the weather

drive the freeway

give CPR

sign up for classes

pick up brother or sister

use a microwave

care for a scratch

call the doctor

call in sick

take temperature

treat a cold or flu

read a road map

read a street map

plan a vacation

make plane reservations

hike 5 miles

make a fire

One Step at a Time

Success Attribute Covered	Proactivity, Goal Setting, Perseverance
Familiarity with Success Attributes	Intermediate lesson
Suggested Grade Level	Grades 3 to 12
Objective(s)	To develop the understanding that one has control over the outcome of one's life
Materials Needed	Worksheet for each student Pens and pencils
Approximate Time	50 minutes

Directions to Implement the Activity	Review the terms of proactivity, goal setting, and perseverance and the steps needed to get a job:
	
	    Some have to be completed first
	    Others have some flexibility but must be done eventually
	    Noting steps helps one feel in control and helps remember what to do
	
	Distribute worksheets and review vocabulary from the lists; discuss the importance of each item and a need for sequence or not
	
	Have students put their lists in order
	
	Share the order of the lists, and discuss why some are different from others
	
	May follow up by asking students if they would change the list for themselves
	
	Ask students to write one or two goals that relate to their personal list
	
	Discuss how perseverance might be needed to accomplish the steps

Suggested Modifications	Complexity may require that students work in small groups May want to categorize or semantically map choices so that students can more clearly see options Encourage students to transfer ideas from the first exercise to the second Students might want to share lists with others in the class
Caveats Regarding Possible Sensitivity of Topic	The fictitious example might be more readily addressed than the exercise that requires students to personalize it Students should be encouraged to make a list using information from the previous list Reinforce those students who are taking new risks

One Step at a Time

Matt is a junior in high school. He is trying to get a part-time job. He made lists of some things he has to do. Help him by numbering, in order, the items in categories A, B, and C.

A. Decide What Kind of Job to Get (put the steps in order)

____ Make a list of things he does well

____ Make a list of things he likes to do

____ List jobs related to what he likes to do

____ List job-related experiences

____ List benefits, downside of each type of job

B. Decide Which Employers to Seek (put the steps in order)

____ List all related job experiences (including volunteer work)

____ Plot his route to work

____ Visit businesses he may want to work for

____ Learn the abbreviations used in classified ads

____ Figure out how much money he can expect to make

____ Find possible work addresses on the map

____ Figure out type of transportation he will need

____ Learn how jobs are listed in the newspaper

____ List the pluses and minuses of the businesses he visits

____ List all employers' good and bad features

____ Choose three or four possible employers

____ Discuss choices with parent(s)

____ Learn the parts of the classified ads

C. Apply for the Job (put the steps in order)

____ Get a Social Security card

____ Brush teeth

____ Dress for success!

____ Put driver's license, work permit, Social Security card in wallet

____ Make a list of past work experience (paid, volunteer)

____ Leave house so he'll be on time

____ Look at road map, plot route to interview

___ Eat breakfast

___ Ask parents for emergency money

___ Get work permit

___ Have list of personal or employment references, or both (phone numbers, addresses, and so forth)

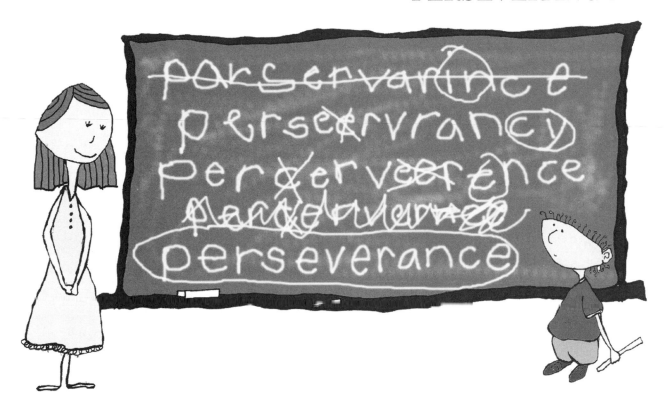

Students who are able to persevere:

- Keep pursuing their goals despite adversity
- Maintain the attitude that difficult situations are necessary learning experiences and that struggle helps improve character and reach goals
- Have a sense of not giving up and learn from hardship
- Know when to quit
- Are flexible in making decisions and pursue alternative avenues of action when necessary
- Find a way around obstacles to their progress

Introduction to Perseverance

Success Attribute Covered	Perseverance
Familiarity with Success Attributes	Introductory lesson
Suggested Grade Level	Grades 3 to 12
Objective(s)	To define perseverance and identify related concepts
Materials Needed	Worksheet for each student Pens and pencils Chalkboard or display board for teacher notes
Approximate Time	50 minutes

Directions to Implement the Activity	Explain how perseverance fits into the Success Attributes
	
	Ask the students to give examples of perseverance from their lives or from people in the news or people they know
	
	List possible terms associated with perseverance (some may surface from their examples):
	
	    Breaking a large task into smaller steps
	    Practicing
	    Identifying the challenges that lead to creating or designing solutions
	    Internal power
	    Taking responsibility for one's own actions
	    Drive to make something better
	
	In small groups, ask students to define perseverance and identify one instance in their life in which perseverance is important

Suggested Modifications	Assist students with writing If small groups are used, assign students to groups based on their willingness to take risks and support one another
Caveats Regarding Possible Sensitivity of Topic	Students will paraphrase or summarize all questions except the final questions (which are applications). They may be frustrated about finding an answer or appear anxious expressing their thoughts.

Introduction to Perseverance

Follow your teacher's instructions for responding to the following items.

1. Explain how perseverance fits into the Success Attributes:

    _____

    _____

    _____

2. Write the definition of the following terms in your own words:

    Making good decisions _____

    _____

    Breaking a large task into smaller steps _____

    _____

    Practicing _____

    _____

    Identifying the challenges that leads to creating or designing solutions _____

    _____

    Internal power _____

    _____

    Taking responsibility for one's own action _____

    _____

    Drive to make something better _____

    _____

3. Write your own definition for *perseverance:*

    _____

    _____

4. Write one instance in your life where perseverance is important:

    _____

    _____

Help by Example

Success Attribute Covered	Perseverance
Familiarity with Success Attributes	Intermediate lesson
Suggested Grade Level	Grades 1 to 12
Objective(s)	To have a sense of not giving up and learning from hardship
Materials Needed	Book (or movie) where a character overcomes obstacle or barrier (see the Children's Literature list in Appendix in A for suggestions) May want to initially use a short biography (of Christopher Reeves, Lance Armstrong, or Stephen Hawkins, *Eleanor Roosevelt*, for example) or a movie Worksheet for each student Pens and pencils
Approximate Time	Depends on length of book or movie and how long students need to complete it
Directions to Implement the Activity	Determine how students will be reading the book: whole class, teacher reads a selection a day, small groups read together, all reading done as homework Select the literature that might best fit the class Revisit the definition of *perseverance* and associated ideas (sticking to completion, relating to meeting a goal, overcoming obstacles, barriers, drawbacks, setbacks) Introduce the idea that literature and characters help students understand perseverance and explain what book will be read and how it will be addressed in future classes Discuss with class (1) the characters, (2) their struggles, (3) other contributing aspects of the story, and (4) predictions for next time Distribute worksheets, and ask students to note ideas about the characters as they read (sections or chapters) As the story continues, note how the characters change; distribute blank worksheets, or ask students to cross out old ideas and add new ones At the end of the activity, the students (working independently or in small groups) should summarize how their key characters persevered: Each student should express how those keys might be used in his or her life by writing either an essay or a short statement

Suggested Modifications	Consider assistive technology (optical character reading, books on tape) for students who struggle with reading but understand the content of passages
	Use of short stories and other media may be more effective for some groups
Caveats Regarding Possible Sensitivity of Topic	Some characters may share more than perseverance with students and may be problematic:
	For instance, if the character has a physical characteristic (short, tall, fat, thin) that is similar to one of the students, additional discussions and difficulty may arise
Adaptability of Lesson to Other Success Attributes	Use the worksheet with other books and success attributes to discuss other characters and their challenges (support systems, emotional coping strategies, goals, self-awareness)

Help by Example

Name of book/movie_____

Name of key character_____

Make notes about the key character at the end of each section.

pp. _____ to pp. _____

_____

_____

_____

pp. _____ to pp. _____

_____

_____

pp. _____ to pp. _____

_____

_____

pp. _____ to pp. _____

_____

_____

_____

pp. _____ to pp. _____

_____

_____

_____

Don't Quit

Success Attribute Covered	Perseverance, Emotional Coping Strategies
Familiarity with Success Attributes	Intermediate lesson
Suggested Grade Level	Grades 5 to 12
Objective(s)	To develop strategies for dealing with obstacles and setbacks and adjusting to change
Materials Needed	Worksheet for each student Pencils and pens Ruler for tracking Chalkboard or area for group Optional index card for each note taking student
Approximate Time	50 minutes
Directions to Implement the Activity	Review the importance of not giving up on a task or goal
	Relate a personal story or a story from someone familiar to the students; if one of the books from the children's literature section (see Appendix A) under perseverance was read, review the theme with the students
	On chalkboard, list reasons that completing a task is important—for example:

	Feeling proud when the job is done
	    Getting the reward
	    Learning from the experience
	    Overcoming obstacles

	After list is complete, discuss that people use strategies to help them get to the end of a task
	Develop a list of strategies (ask, "What strategies would you suggest?") a person might try before quitting or might do to get the job completed
	Record ideas on the board while the students are encouraged to record the responses on their worksheets
	When list is developed, students put a star in front of the strategies they have not tried
	Ask or assign students to record the date each time they attempt to use a strategy during the week, reporting back after three days
	Put list in the front of the student's binder (or students can reproduce the list on an index card, marking dates to the side of the strategy)
	Follow up with a discussion of when and how a strategy was used and why a strategy might not have been used; do this daily for three days, then a couple of times a week for a semester

	Might survey to see if other strategies were tried that should be added to the list
Suggested Modifications	Assist students with the writing task
	Provide the students with the class list from which they could identify the tried and never-tried tasks
	Assist students in recording their answer
	Use icons, magazine pictures, photos, and stickers to symbolize a task to try
Caveats Regarding Possible Sensitivity of Topic	May address some emotionally-charged issues for the student
	Select one or two strategies from the class list after a conference with individual students to avoid overwhelming them and help them work on specific goals
	Check with more sensitive students if they wish to present to the class to avoid the shock of surprise. Encourage less talkative students to share their ideas by helping them prepare or practice before presenting to the group.
	Acknowledge all for their attempts, noting the challenge and risk of trying something new
	Commend for any change, additionally noting the circumstances where they tried any strategies they might not have tried in the past

Don't Quit

Directions: Perseverance is keeping at a task until it is finished. It takes emotional strength and practice. This worksheet provides strategies to help persevere. Three are listed to help you get started. Then list six more alternatives to quitting, and put a star beside the ones you have never tried before. Mark the date in the right column each time you use that strategy.

Things to Do Instead of Quitting	I Tried It!
Take a break	_____
Listen to a song I like	_____
Talk it over with a friend	_____
_____	_____
_____	_____
_____	_____
_____	_____
_____	_____
_____	_____

Help with Hanging in There

Success Attribute Covered	Perseverance, Support Systems
Familiarity with Success Attributes	Intermediate lesson; may use as a follow-up activity to "Don't Quit"
Suggested Grade Level	Grades 1 to 12
Objective(s)	To develop strategies for dealing with obstacles and setbacks, and adjusting to change
Materials Needed	Worksheet Pens and pencils Craft materials to make posters and drawings Camcorders (if available) for student commercials
Approximate Time	90 minutes
Directions to Implement the Activity	Review or create strategies that people use when they feel like quitting—for example: Get help or information Try some other way Get encouragement from family or friends Do something else for a while Make a mental picture of success Give self a pep talk Explain the assignment: In time allotted, students work either alone or in pairs or small groups to design a billboard, commercial, or magazine ad to encourage people to try one of the strategies from the list Purpose of advertisements is to see the strategy and get people interested in it Students will complete the worksheet and get teacher approval prior to creating the advertisement When the advertisement is completed, students will present their creations to the class Share commonalities and differences among the projects while reinforcing the importance of using strategies and helping others find alternatives to quitting
Suggested Modifications	May want to limit alternatives of presentation (for example, everyone draws a picture) Assign working partners by considering how much risk taking students will do with one another

	Students might be grouped according to the contribution they can make to each group (such that not all good artists are in the same group)
Caveats Regarding Possible Sensitivity of Topic	Selection of topic by the group may be difficult, as might the means to advertise it
	While students are sharing their preliminary worksheet, question them about specifics of accomplishing the assignment:
	Who will do what How much time is needed for each step

Help with Hanging in There

Directions: Design a commercial or billboard or magazine ad to encourage people to try your strategy when they want to quit.

Which strategy are you advertising?

_____

_____

What else do you want to say or write about the strategy?

_____

_____

What else do you need to draw, find, or write to finish your advertisement?

_____

_____

Playing Games and Persevering

Success Attribute Covered	Perseverance, Self-Awareness, Emotional Coping
Familiarity with Success Attributes	Intermediate lesson
Suggested Grade Level	Grades 1 to 12
Objective(s)	To maintain the attitude that difficult situations are necessary learning experiences and struggles will help build character and reach goals

Materials Needed	Games
	  Board
	  Cards
	  Access to gym or playground
	  equipment outdoors
	
	Worksheet for each student
	Pencils and pens

Approximate Time	90 minutes over two sessions
Directions to Implement the Activity	Review concepts related to perseverance, emotions, self-awareness. For instance, sometimes when completing a task, our emotions affect our attitude negatively or positively Typically, a positive attitude can lead to a task where one feels accomplished, good, and happy A negative attitude might mean the task was a struggle, difficult, may or may not be completed satisfactorily, generally leaving the individual feeling low, cranky, sad Checking for good attitude might mean that even a difficult task is done easily To help with this idea, the class is going to practice monitoring how they feel while playing some games (board games, card games, physical games) The first task is to complete a survey independently to determine which games will be played and when: Some modifications of the games may be needed so there are enough people to play each game Any response will be limited by the kinds of games that are available Schedule students to play one of the games in each of their four categories After 10 minutes of play, students will independently answer the questions They will continue this until all four games are played

	After final responses are complete, volunteers can share their reactions regarding attitude and perseverance
	Revisiting related concepts from beginning of session should be the focus
Suggested Modifications	The physical education instructor may be willing to help with the playground games during scheduled physical education class
	This activity will require a substantial collection of games, so that student choice is possible; a prewritten list may be needed for student reference
	Some students may need to be reminded the purpose of the activity is to think about perseverance and not about winning the game
Caveats Regarding Possible Sensitivity of Topic	Scheduling students so that all have two positive and two negative experiences
	Because of scheduling issues, students may be playing games with challenging individuals
	Close monitoring might be needed
	If possible, student might bring games from home
	Video games may or may not be an option depending on your resources and willingness to have them at school

Playing Games and Persevering

Games I Like

_____

_____

_____

Games I Am Good At

_____

_____

_____

Games I Don't Like

_____

_____

_____

Games I Struggle With

_____

_____

_____

Play the game for 10 minutes. After each game, answer these questions.

First Game

How I felt while playing the game

_____

_____

If I felt negative, what could I do the next time to change my attitude?

_____

_____

If I felt positive, how could I use those feelings the next time in a different game?

_____

Second Game

How I felt while playing the game

_____

_____

If I felt negative, what could I do the next time to change my attitude?

_____

_____

If I felt positive, could I use those feelings the next time in a different game?

_____

Third Game

How I felt while playing the game

_____

_____

If I felt negative, what could I do the next time to change my attitude?

_____

_____

If I felt positive, could I use those feelings the next time in a different game?

_____

Fourth Game

How did I feel while playing the game?

_____

_____

If I felt negative, what could I do the next time to change my attitude?

_____

_____

If I felt positive, could I use those feelings the next time in a different game?

_____

Perseverance Award

Success Attribute Covered	Perseverance
Familiarity with Success Attributes	Intermediate lesson
Suggested Grade Level	Grades 1 to 12
Objective(s)	To recognize that passion and desire keep one moving
Materials Needed	Worksheet for identified students
Approximate Time	5 minutes
Directions to Implement the Activity	This award can be used in a variety of ways: At the end of a difficult activity (project, test, assignment), all students receive the award as completed by the teacher At the end of a difficulty activity, all students complete their own award, acknowledging their own work After a specific student completes a difficult assignment despite the odds, the teacher completes the award and presents it to the student individually The key to the award is the specific acknowledgment on the final line, which personalizes it for the student relative to perseverance and students' passions or desires
Suggested Modifications	Discuss award with student to check his or her understanding
Caveats Regarding Possible Sensitivity of Topic	Be aware of students' sensitivity to public recognition

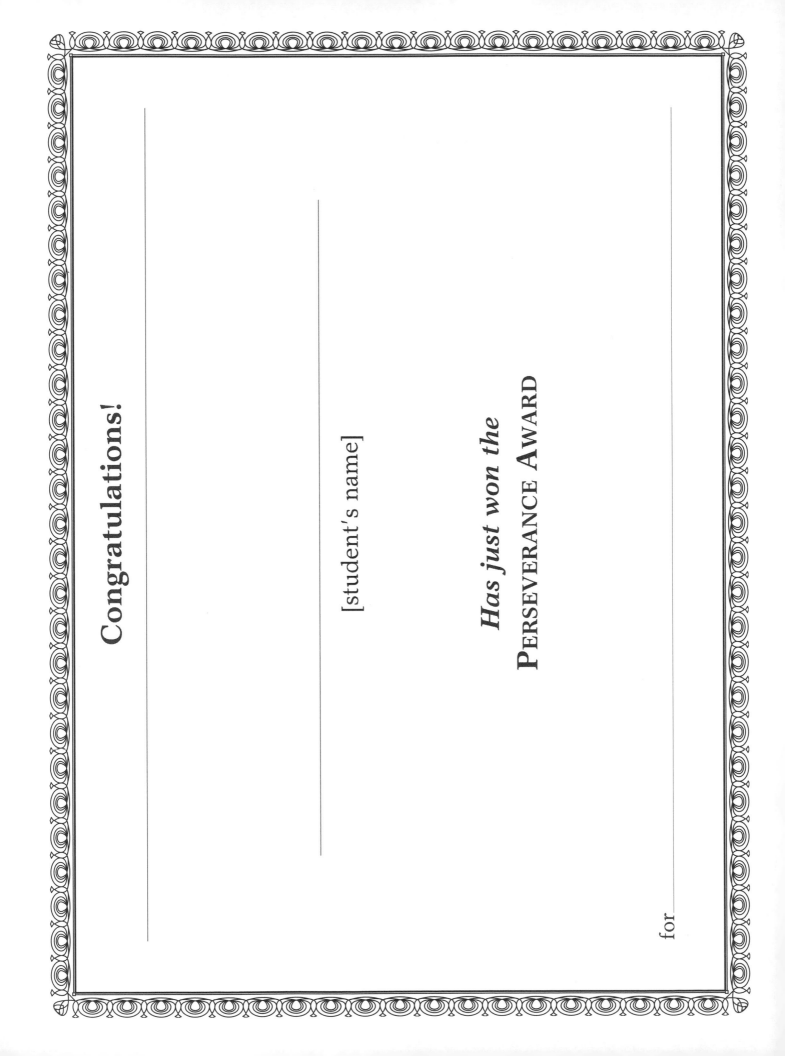

Congratulations!

[student's name]

Has just won the
PERSEVERANCE AWARD

for

Work It Out! Hold On to That Job!

Success Attribute Covered	Perseverance
Familiarity with Success Attributes	Advanced lesson
Suggested Grade Level	Grades 3 to 12
Objective(s)	To understand perseverance as it relates to goal setting
Materials Needed	Worksheet Pens and pencils Ruler or index card to track responses Overhead display of worksheet
Approximate Time	50 minutes
Directions to Implement the Activity	Ask students to give ideas about what is important to get and keep a job: If they have difficulty answering, discuss what seems to be so important in school that there are rules for things (being on time, dressing appropriately) Explain that workplaces have rules (written and unwritten) that need to be followed for employees to keep their jobs. Distribute the worksheet, and ask students to complete the first five items as a group before they work independently In the first column, students should check if they can do that item today In the second column, they should mark the age at which they should be able to do the task (that age may be younger than the students are currently) The third column allows students to rank how important they think an item is to maintaining a job (1 = low, 5 = high) For closure, discuss how these skills relate to perseverance
Suggested Modifications	For younger students, select a few items to discuss at one time; may want to select those that can be part of a goal for the class now: For instance, being on time, dress appropriately, clean hands, face, and body might be a focus of the class, so selecting the first three to five items of the worksheet for discussion and then recalling those items throughout the week might be helpful

Given students' responses to any item, more class time might be needed to elaborate on specifics (for example, "good manners, know your rights"); this may be age-dependent

As part of the discussion in math, the rankings might be tallied to find the mean, median, and mode for the class

Caveats Regarding Possible Sensitivity of Topic	May need to strongly emphasize that people can have differing opinions of the tasks and skills presented
	In addition, students might need reminders that the skills listed include many kinds of skills, some of which may not be part of any one job
	Students may need a reminder at the beginning of this class to maintain a respectful attitude toward others' comments

Work It Out! Hold On to That Job!

Directions: In the first column, check the item you do now. In the second column, put the age you will be when you can do what the item says. In the third column, rate how important the item is or might be to you. A 1 means not very important. A 5 means very important.

As of Now, I CAN!	At This Age, I WILL!	How Important I Think This Is (rate on a scale of 1 to 5)
____ Be on time	_____	_____
____ Dress appropriately	_____	_____
____ Clean hands, face, hair, body	_____	_____
____ Have tools I need	_____	_____
____ Conform to uniform or dress code	_____	_____
____ Be serious and alert	_____	_____
____ Be courteous to coworkers	_____	_____
____ Don't curse	_____	_____
____ Finish work when due	_____	_____
____ Don't talk back to customers	_____	_____
____ Do what the boss says	_____	_____
____ Don't argue with the boss	_____	_____
____ Know what's safe, dangerous	_____	_____
____ Know my rights	_____	_____
____ Know boss's expectations	_____	_____
____ Don't be upset, angry	_____	_____
____ Don't steal, cheat, or lie	_____	_____

Perseverance

Occupations, Job Searching

Success Attribute Covered	Perseverance
Familiarity with Success Attributes	Intermediate lesson
Suggested Grade Level	Grades 3 to 12
Objective(s)	To be flexible in making decisions to pursue other avenues in response to action
Materials Needed	Worksheet for each student Pens and pencils Chalkboard Overhead of worksheet Classified ad listing jobs from newspaper or newspaper Web sites
Approximate Time	30 minutes
Directions to Implement the Activity	Review concepts related to perseverance and the importance of having options available for good decision making Introduce the idea that when searching for a job, the newspaper may be one avenue among many for job-seeking possibilities Group students, and ask that they list jobs found in the classified sections that they have at their desks When they have a complete list from the classifieds written in the first column, ask them to list occupations they might choose that are not listed in newspaper For each of those listed, ask them to think about how they might find out about that job When each group is finished, gather worksheets and compile the results Discuss why jobs may be listed in the newspaper and why others may be listed in other places Ask the group to tell what job searching has to do with perseverance
Suggested Modifications	Because the jobs are listed alphabetically, group students so that each group will have either the same (or different) lists; within a limited time, compare the lists that the students compile May need to have a list of occupations available for students to reference once they have looked at the classified ads Prior to the lesson, teacher or students can survey parents, other people students know for their thoughts about jobs and how they are found
Caveats Regarding Possible Sensitivity of Topic	Seeking input from family members may be difficult Students may have limited knowledge of jobs

Occupations, Job Searching

Directions: In the first column, write the jobs found in the classified section of the newspaper. In the second column, write the jobs you might want that are not listed. In the third column, note how you might find apply for those jobs,

In the Newspaper	Not in the Newspaper	How to Find Out About This Job
Accountant _____	Ballerina _____	Get an agent, audition _____
_____	_____	_____
_____	_____	_____
_____	_____	_____
_____	_____	_____
_____	_____	_____
_____	Firefighter _____	Apply at city hall _____
_____	_____	_____
_____	_____	_____
_____	_____	_____
_____	_____	_____
_____	_____	_____
_____	_____	_____
_____	_____	_____

After-School Goals

Success Attribute Covered	**Perseverance, Goal Setting, Proactivity**
Familiarity with Success Attributes	Advanced lesson
Suggested Grade Level	Grades 3 to 12
Objective(s)	To understand perseverance as it relates to goal setting
Materials Needed	Worksheet for each student Pens and pencils
Approximate Time	50 minutes initially 50 minutes for checking progress

Directions to Implement the Activity	Define and introduce each of the six areas listed on worksheet:
	
	    Can be addressed outside school
	    Encompass much of our lives
	
	Review terms associated with perseverance and setting good goals
	
	Ask students to select a number of the areas (dependent on the age and sophistication of group) and write one goal for each of the areas that can be met within a specific time (so that updates about progress can be checked)
	
	Students should design a graph or means for monitoring progress toward the goal
	
	Students should agree to meet the goals that are set, noting a realistic plan of action, and identify how perseverance is needed to help meet the goal
	
	Discuss what else a person might need to persevere with the goal
	
	The class might agree to check on each other's progress and determine when those checks will be accomplished

Suggested Modifications	Limit discussion and definition of domains to similar terms Reduce the number of goals to write and track to one or two Assist with writing and graphing
Caveats Regarding Possible Sensitivity of Topic	Students may be reluctant to identify a goal that attends to a weakness Students may have difficulty establishing a goal in an area (because of where a student lives, she or he may be unable to do community service) May need to have a teacher brainstorm some creative pathways to set a goal and identify ways to persevere

The Six Success Factors for Children with Learning Disabilities

After-School Goals

Directions: Write one personal goal and some ways to help persevere for each one.

1. Physical self goal (sports, health, appearance)

   _____

   Ways to persevere:

   _____

   _____

2. Social self goal (family relationships, friends, group membership)

   _____

   Ways to persevere:

   _____

   _____

3. Emotional self goal (coping with stress, problem behaviors, new behaviors)

   _____

   Ways to persevere:

   _____

   _____

4. Artistic self goal (visual arts, music, dance, writing/storytelling)

   _____

   Ways to persevere:

   _____

   _____

5. Community/public self goal (helping others or the community, participating in activities)

   _____

Ways to persevere:

_____

_____

6. Spiritual self goal (religious beliefs, right and wrong behaviors)

_____

Ways to persevere:

_____

_____

Long-Range Plans

Success Attribute Covered	**Perseverance, Goal Setting, Proactivity**
Familiarity with Success Attributes	Intermediate lesson
Suggested Grade Level	Grades 3 to 12
Objective(s)	To understand that goals need to be specific yet flexible to take advantage of the opportunity To practice keeping goals despite diversity
Materials Needed	Worksheet for each student Pens and pencils Book (or other materials identified in goal)
Approximate Time	50 minutes initially 5-minute checks of progress frequently

Directions to Implement the Activity	Review terms and the importance of setting goals to persevere:
	
	    Explain that long-term goals usually comprise a set of short-term subgoals, objectives, and steps; provide an example
	    Explain that perseverance is necessary to meet long-term goals; achieving little steps helps perseverance
	    One helpful way to monitor progress is to set up weekly or even daily subgoals or steps and then evaluate the progress, for example, by using weekly graphs
	
	Challenge students to practice setting appropriate goals for themselves; remind them that perseverance is needed to help meet goals
	
	Present and explain worksheet
	
	Select books, materials, and assignments to be used to set goal
	
	Have each student complete a rough draft of at least one goal
	
	Share goals and other strategies to persevere with group; congratulate group for setting appropriate goals

Suggested Modifications	Students may need help with graphing and recording progress May need to pair students for assistance, reminders Teachers will need to make sure that goals and steps are attainable for each student and long enough to discuss perseverance
Caveats Regarding Possible Sensitivity of Topic	Students may need help selecting, establishing, and staying focused on goal A system of frequent checks and rewards (acknowledgments) from the teacher may help students persevere

Long-Range Plans

Directions: Set a big *general* goal for yourself at school. Write what it is and when you need to finish it—your target date. Then think of three steps that are a part of the general goal. In order to ensure your success in reaching your big goal, you need to persevere and monitor its progress. Write what you need to do each week for each step.

Example

Subject:	Reading
General Goal:	Do book report
To be completed by	(Target date): January 31
Step Number	Subgoal
1	Read ½ chapter per day Monday through Friday
2	Each day make notes about events of book
3	Write draft of book report two days before it is due

Subject: _____

General goal: _____

Target date: _____

Step Number	Subgoal	Date Completed
1	_____	_____
2	_____	_____
3	_____	_____

Other things I need to do to persevere to accomplish this goal:

_____

_____

chapter four
GOAL SETTING

Students with strong goal-setting skills:

- Identify their goals early on
- Show evidence of planning skills
- Establish a step-by-step process to reach each goal
- Set goals that tend to:
  - Be realistic and attainable
  - Provide direction and meaning to their lives
  - Be specific yet flexible enough to take advantage of opportunities that arise
  - Cover multiple domains
  - Become identified in early adolescence

87

Introduction to Goal Setting

Success Attribute Covered	Goal Setting
Familiarity with Success Attributes	Introductory lesson
Suggested Grade Level	Grades 3 to 12
Objective(s)	To define goals and related concepts
Materials Needed	Worksheet for each student Chalkboard and chalk OR display board Poster paper and markers to record students' responses
Approximate Time	1 hour

Directions to Implement the Activity	Provide situations where setting a goal made someone's life better, successful, or easier:
	
	    Example: Big project for school or work that must be completed in two weeks
	
	Elicit suggestions from the group about what can be done; ask group to write notes on worksheets
	
	Ask group for other suggestions about similar events in their lives (worksheet)
	
	Define *goal setting* and related terms:
	
	    Ability to set specific yet flexible goals in a number of domains
	    Ability to modify goals
	    Setting goals that are realistic and attainable
	
	Ask group to suggest all or parts of goals from examples in their lives
	
	May want to introduce a long-term project here and model how to break a large assignment into manageable and short-term goals

Suggested Modifications	Have available a variety of examples (following a recipe or game rules, finishing a sewing task) Might need a list of related terms
Caveats Regarding Possible Sensitivity of Topic	Unless examples have some sensitivity, goal setting may be free of emotions for most students

Introduction to Goal Setting

Directions: Write notes from class here.

1. What is a goal?

   _____

   _____

2. Why do you need goals?

   _____

   _____

3. When is it a good idea to set a goal?

   _____

   _____

4. When is it okay not to set a goal?

   _____

   _____

5. What would happen if you don't set a goal when you need one?

   _____

   _____

6. List parts of goal:

   _____   _____

   _____   _____

   _____   _____

7. Give an example of a goal:

   _____

Plan a Party

Success Attribute Covered	**Goal Setting, Social Support Systems, Proactivity**
Familiarity with Success Attributes	Introductory lesson
Suggested Grade Level	Grades 1 to 12
Objective(s)	To develop strategies for goal setting, working with others, and prioritizing goals
Materials Needed	Worksheet for each student Pens and pencils Display board or chalkboard Materials for party (see completed worksheet)
Approximate Time	45 minutes to plan
Directions to Implement the Activity	Implement this lesson several weeks prior to an appropriate date for a party Introduce the lesson by hypothesizing what a person does to have a party, asking for information from the group Divide the students into groups of three or four: Each group discusses and then completes the worksheet for the party After checking for accuracy of information, post the plans and allow time for groups to vote on their favorite idea Once the class has selected the plan, divide and assign prioritized goals to entire class Assign duties to students (who will bring specific supplies; confirm dates) Schedule party Hold party Meet after the party to discuss the strengths and weaknesses of goal setting for events
Suggested Modifications	Students who do not want to participate should be given either a written or oral (use tape recorder) task to explain why they do not wish to participate and what they will do during the party rather than attend May want students to cut out pictures from catalogues as alternative to writing
Caveats Regarding Possible Sensitivity of Topic	Students may need some lessons and practice working in groups, expressing ideas, and accepting others' ideas Monitor or set limits regarding party theme

Plan a Party

Directions: Brainstorm ideas for a party, and have one person in your group record the ideas.

1. Our theme is _____

   _____

2. Party favors that will match the theme _____

   _____

3. Decorations that will match the theme _____

   _____

4. What the invitations should say and look like to match the theme _____

   _____

5. Foods that match the theme _____

   _____

6. Three activities that match the theme

   a. _____

   _____

   b. _____

   _____

   c. _____

   _____

7. Our list of what needs to be done (food cooked, put up decorations, and so on), who will do it, and the date when each should be done.

Thing to Be Done	By Whom	By When
_____	_____	_____
_____	_____	_____
_____	_____	_____
_____	_____	_____

Shop 'til You Drop

Success Attribute Covered	Goal Setting, Perseverance
Familiarity with Success Attributes	Intermediate lesson
Suggested Grade Level	Grades 1 to 12
Objective(s)	To develop action plans and steps for reaching goals
Materials Needed	Worksheet for each student Pens and pencils Catalogues, newspapers, Internet (for prices of items)
Approximate Time	50 minutes

Directions to Implement the Activity	Review with students the terms of goal setting (step-by-step, realistic, specific)
	
	Introduce goal setting as related to buying something
	
	Model concept through buying a car (or some other purchase in their future):
	
	    Research cars to determine what would be best for their need
	    Determine how much money is involved
	    Determine how much money is available
	    Determine options for where to purchase
	
	Ask students to select five items they want and pick one:
	
	    For that item, student should record all steps necessary to purchase item
	    When students are finished, review a couple of examples from the class, and discuss importance of setting goals using terms previously discussed
	
	Ask students for an indication about their interest in and usefulness of this exercise

Suggested Modifications	Place students into groups of three or four to help with tasks Limit items purchased to smaller, readily attainable items (might involve fewer steps)
Caveats Regarding Possible Sensitivity of Topic	Students may be unable to separate the exercise from the reality Discussion about practice versus reality may be necessary Stress that this is an exercise for discussion, not for actually buying the items

Shop 'til You Drop

Five Things I'd Like to Buy   **The Cost**

_____   _____

_____   _____

_____   _____

_____   _____

_____   _____

Put a star next to one of the items for which you would be willing to do ALL the steps to purchase it. Then list the steps needed.

Steps I Must Take to Get the Starred Item

_____

_____

_____

_____

_____

School Tour

Success Attribute Covered	Goal Setting
Familiarity with Success Attributes	Introductory lesson
Suggested Grade Level	Grades 3 to 12
Objective(s)	Understand that goals are realistic and attainable
Materials Needed	Worksheet for each student Pens and pencils
Approximate Time	50 minutes
Directions to Implement the Activity	Discuss the importance of planning, being realistic, being specific, and doing something attainable (necessary components of goal setting) Explain that one way to practice these terms is to think about giving a tour of the school Ask students to complete the worksheet by selecting anywhere to begin, but maintain an order and map of how to tour the school: 　　Indicate which rooms or areas the group will see 　　Explain how the area or room is used 　　Explain whom they may encounter in any given area, the title of that person, and what questions they might ask that individual When completed, examine several tours as a group Establish that each began at a different place but evaluate by checking if tour was complete, specific, attainable, realistic Review terms relating the assignment completed to goal setting
Suggested Modifications	Work in pairs (teacher assigned) May need help recording Accuracy may need monitoring May need to reduce size of assignment—for instance, touring only cafeteria or playground
Caveats Regarding Possible Sensitivity of Topic	Little sensitivity unless student is totally unacquainted with school or demonstrates anxiety over how to begin a lesson this complex

School Tour

Directions: Complete the sections as directed by the teacher.

Rooms or Areas to Tour	How Room or Area Is Used
_____	_____
_____	_____
_____	_____
_____	_____

People We Might Meet

Name	Location	Questions to Ask This Person
_____	_____	_____
_____	_____	_____
_____	_____	_____
_____	_____	_____
_____	_____	_____
_____	_____	_____
_____	_____	_____
_____	_____	_____
_____	_____	_____
_____	_____	_____

Book Report

Success Attribute Covered	Goal Setting
Familiarity with Success Attributes	Intermediate lesson
Suggested Grade Level	Grades 2 to 12
Objective(s)	To apply step-by-step process to a real goal
Materials Needed	Worksheet for each student Calendar Sticky notes Calculators Book student is to read for report Student planner
Approximate Time	30 minutes with 15-minute follow-up

Directions to Implement the Activity	Each student must select book prior to session
	
	Due date for completion is clearly identified
	
	Students mark the due date in their planners and on their worksheets
	
	Teacher notes due date on large monthly calendar that is or will be displayed in class
	
	Each student determines how long it will take to complete report:
	
	    Subtract the number of days to complete report from the total number of days (using worksheet steps)
	    Determine how many days are needed to read the book (students will need to consider their scheduled family time, parties, and other events)
	    Determine the number of chapters or sections or pages in the book and divides that number by the number of days needed to read the book
	
	Students write the number of chapters or pages they must read daily in their planners
	
	Ask students what happens if they read more than the required sections (they finish early)
	
	Ask students what happens if they do not read according to the plan (they fall behind):
	
	    Brainstorm some possible plans if they fall behind schedule (read more the following days, for example)
	
	Emphasize that a portion of their grade will depend on timely completion
	
	Check periodically on students' progress

Suggested Modifications	Might introduce this process by having the whole class read the same book, modeling each step above, or reviewing past books or projects
	Students may individually modify the reading schedule based on their own activities
Caveats Regarding Possible Sensitivity of Topic	Some students may need individual conferencing to stay on track with the project
	If grades or points are assigned, clearly specify consequences for incomplete work

Book Report

Checklist for Completion

Title of book _____

Book report is due _____

Days needed to write book report _____

Number of pages or chapters in book _____ (*hint:* divide total pages or chapters into even parts)

Sections or chapters ÷ number of days to read = _____

Amount to read each day _____

Put the daily assignment in your planner (for example, "Monday: read Chapter 1; Tuesday: read Chapter 2").

Criminal Investigation

Success Attribute Covered	Goal Setting, Perseverance
Familiarity with Success Attributes	Introductory lesson
Suggested Grade Level	Grades 4 to 12
Objective(s)	To develop strategies for reevaluating and overcoming obstacles
Materials Needed	Worksheet for each student Pens and pencils Envelopes for clues
Approximate Time	One to five class sessions (10 minutes each)
Directions to Implement the Activity	Teacher removes an item of value from the classroom Teacher reveals two clues each day (or all in one long session) about the items Possible clues: "It was not what was in the room, but what was *not* in the room." "There was never any doubt who did it, but how it was done." "What the suspect wore on the day of the crime was important." "The person didn't mean to reveal that he or she committed the crime, but that's what he or she did." "The suspect actually told me that everyone knows who committed the crime; we just failed to understand him or her." Students discuss in groups possible solutions to the crime, creating their own tree of possibilities (see the worksheet) Make a tree of possibilities incorporating all suggested solutions and relations to the crime Students make predictions and secure them in envelopes After all envelopes are collected, teacher reveals how the crime was committed Teacher writes key points of crime on board Teacher compared predictions with actual crime facts Students use worksheet to describe the crime and solution in their own words Discuss goal-setting concepts as related to remaining flexible
Suggested Modifications	Alternatives to writing may be necessary; structuring questions and responses for students with language processing difficulty may be needed
Caveats Regarding Possible Sensitivity of Topic	Students may have difficulty separating this activity from reality, so monitoring student reactions will be important

Criminal Investigation

Tree of Possibilities

On the branches of the tree, write the clues. On the trunk of the tree, write the possible solutions.

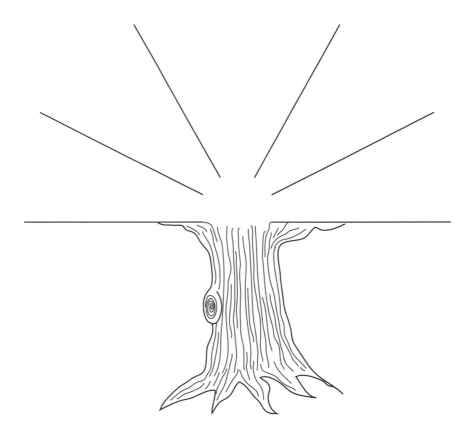

In your own words, describe the scenario and discuss how you came to your conclusion.

_____

The Six Success Factors for Children with Learning Disabilities

Where I Am and Where I Want to Be

Success Attribute Covered	Goal Setting, Self-Awareness
Familiarity with Success Attributes	Introductory lesson
Suggested Grade Level	Grades 2 to 12
Objective(s)	To use goals for planning now and in the future
Materials Needed	Worksheet for each student Pictures from magazines Scissors, glue, blank paper Pens and pencils
Approximate Time	50 minutes
Directions to Implement the Activity	Review concepts related to goal setting from introductory discussion: specific, long and short term, realistic
	Suggest that goal setting is personal and takes place in all aspects of a student's life: home, school, community, and other aspects
	Explain that students should think about themselves today, develop with the class the categories that might be considered (after-school activities, likes or dislikes, food, clothing, friends, family, cars, jobs, subjects in school), and list their responses on worksheets
	Select a time in the future (1, 2, 5, 10 years), and ask students to consider the same categories and list responses on their worksheets:
	Note that answers are for discussion and should be as realistic as possible
	Distribute blank paper (size may depend on time spent on project), and ask students to draw a dotted line down the middle of the page
	Explain that students will either draw or paste pictures that represent their present on the left side of the page and their future on the right side of the page:
	Students should use their notes from worksheets
	As students are sharing at the end, explain that the dotted line is meant to represent the possible commonalities; where they are at one point in time might have an impact on where they are later:
	After students volunteer their answers, ask the group to consider how realistic these visions are

Ask students to generate a list, either individually or in small groups, about the in-between steps:

> What needs to be done in the time between now and the future to make the two halves come together
>
> Discuss the importance of frequently asking, "What is important to me now?"
>
> Ask students to give examples of what is important now and how that might or might not help accomplish their goals

Students should write one goal for the future

Suggested Modifications	Rather than magazines, have an assortment of pictures precut in several categories (families, sports, jobs, houses, vacations, food, pets) for student selection
	Place specific time limits on each step of the project: time to (1) plan, (2) select pictures or draw, (3) arrange and complete poster
	Use the worksheet as a map, and have students complete the final collage on large paper
	Have students work in small groups to find and select pictures once individual ideas are finished
Caveats Regarding Possible Sensitivity of Topic	May give teacher insight as to how realistic a student is about future goals (depending on the length of time between the two situations)
	Additional individual counseling and discussion may be needed with the student and family about the future

Where I Am and Where I Want to Be

Directions: Under "Where I Am," write qualities you have, what you can do, what you like today. Under "Where I Want to Be," write qualities you want, things you would like to do, places you would like to go in the future.

Where I Am

Good student

Where I Want to Be

Graduate from high school/college

Write one goal for the future:

_____

_____

Road Map to Success

Success Attribute Covered	Goal Setting, Perseverance
Familiarity with Success Attributes	Intermediate lesson
Suggested Grade Level	Grades 4 to 12
Objective(s)	To develop strategies for goal setting
Materials Needed	Worksheet for each student Pens and pencils Chalkboard
Approximate Time	50 minutes over two sessions
Directions to Implement the Activity	Define goals and related terms: *specific, measurable, observable, attainable, realistic, timely* Model writing an example goal (for example, purchasing a video game) Ask students to think of three goals they would like to meet within a very short time During the second session, ask students to have their goals available, and list obstacles that might prevent them from reaching the goals List those obstacles on the board Ask students to select one of their goals and complete the worksheet, providing specific steps, time to accomplish goals, obstacles, and so on list within arrows conditions and if support systems or other strategies are needed Challenge students to meet their individual goals Periodically check with them on their progress
Suggested Modifications	Help students understand examples of terms—for instance, what verbs are measurable and what is a very short time Monitor students' goal selection for realism and timeliness. Students with least understanding might struggle the most with writing a goal that meets all of the requirements.
Caveats Regarding Possible Sensitivity of Topic	Sensitivity to others' goals and abilities

The Six Success Factors for Children with Learning Disabilities

Road Map to Success

Directions

1. Choose one goal, and write it in the star.
2. Begin with the blank arrow above "You are here," and write the first step to reaching the goal.
3. In the next arrow, write the second step.
4. At the octagon, write one obstacle that might stop you from reaching the goal.
5. In the arrow that follows, write one way to overcome the obstacle.
6. In the arrow pointing at the star goal, write the final step to reaching it.

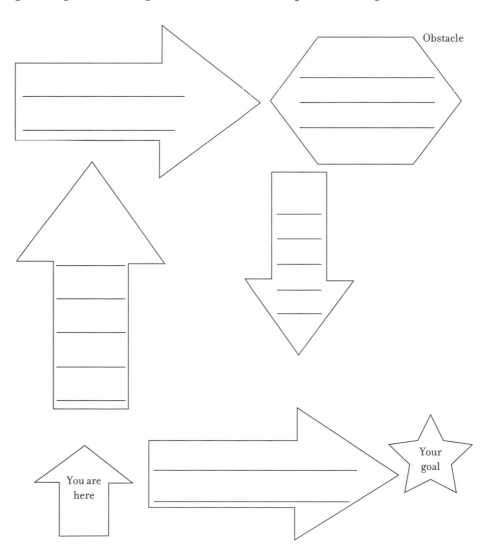

Step-by-Step to Achievement

Success Attribute Covered	Goal Setting
Familiarity with Success Attributes	Intermediate lesson
Suggested Grade Level	Grades 1 to 12
Objective(s)	To understand that goals cover multiple domains
Materials Needed	Worksheet for each student Pens and pencils
Approximate Time	40 minutes
Directions to Implement the Activity	Review ideas from previous lessons on goal setting, highlighting specific vocabulary (short- and long-term, steps, realistic, and the others) that may have presented challenges or were new to students in previous lessons, purpose of goal setting (helps with accomplishing dreams, assignments) Distribute worksheet and explain the instructions Allow time for students to ask clarifying questions Model how to answer one of the questions, and ask students to complete the remainder independently When students have completed their responses, revisit the introductory concepts and objectives; ask students for feedback about the assignments—what goal was the easiest, what goal might be included next time
Suggested Modifications	Help some students record responses accurately in appropriate places Ask students to complete only one or two scenarios at a time Change goals for immediacy or relevance, if needed: For instance, "have a car" might be "have a toy or video game" instead
Caveats Regarding Possible Sensitivity of Topic	Students may need to understand the reality of some questions over others Might need to modify examples to something within their lives

The Six Success Factors for Children with Learning Disabilities

Step-by-Step to Achievement

What if you left your car keys inside your car? What would your goal be? That's right! To find a way to open the car! And there are several ways to do it. Can you think of one of them?

_____

_____

Below are several situations. Please identify a *goal* for each one, along with several *possible ways to reach the goal*.

You lost your homework:

Possible Goals	Is It Long Term (L) or Short Term (S)?	Steps to Reach the Goal
		1 _____
		2 _____
		3 _____

You want to go to Italy:

Possible Goals	Is It Long Term (L) or Short Term (S)?	Steps to Reach the Goal
		1 _____
		2 _____
		3 _____

You want your own car:

Possible Goals	Is It Long Term (L) or Short Term (S)?	Steps to Reach the Goal
		1 _____
		2 _____
		3 _____

You enjoy computers or art so much that you want to do it all the time when you are older:

Possible Goals	Is It Long Term (L) or Short Term (S)?	Steps to Reach the Goal
		1 _____
		2 _____
		3 _____

You need to finish reading a long book by the end of the month:

Possible Goals	Is It Long Term (L) Or Short Term (S)?	Steps to Reach the Goal
		1 _____
		2 _____
		3 _____

What Do I Know About Me?

Success Attribute Covered	Goal Setting
Familiarity with Success Attributes	Intermediate lesson
Suggested Grade Level	Grades 3 to 12
Objective(s)	To understand that goals provide direction and meaning in life
Materials Needed	Worksheet for each student Pens and pencils Chalkboard
Approximate Time	45 minutes
Directions to Implement the Activity	May want to use each time a report card or portfolio feedback or any major progress reporting information is distributed Explain that teacher's feedback (grades, reporting) is based on what students demonstrate and what is observed as effort Brainstorm with students specific information about what grading and reporting shows, and record on board Distribute worksheets and review the vocabulary Students complete responses If possible, distribute report cards or progress information, and ask students to compare their responses with the report Brainstorm possible reasons for discrepancies Ask students to identify one goal to work toward for next reporting time
Suggested Modifications	Students with limited spelling or language may need a list of vocabulary to use to complete the assignment Some students may need additional clarification of language, assistance with writing Limit selection of questions to assist with students' understanding
Caveats Regarding Possible Sensitivity of Topic	Some students will need additional time and counsel to acknowledge their progress and achievement Some students may need guidance to identify realistic progress

What Do I Know About Me?

Directions: Use this sheet for weekly, monthly, or semester review.

1. What my GRADES tell me about what I know:

Facts, skills learned

_____

_____

Assignments completed

_____

_____

Effort

_____

_____

Best, worst subjects, skills

_____

_____

2. What my PORTFOLIO tells me about what I know:

Progress in skills

_____

_____

Development of talents

_____

_____

Development of abilities

_____

_____

Development of special interests

_____

_____

Concepts Learned   Talents Developed

_____   _____

_____   _____

_____   _____

Interests Pursued   Abilities Shown

_____   _____

_____   _____

_____   _____

My goal is: _____

_____

I will meet it by:

_____

_____

chapter five

SOCIAL SUPPORT SYSTEMS

Students with strong social support systems:

- Actively seek out support, guidance, and encouragement from significant others
- Are willing to accept support when offered
- Actively maintain contact with significant others over course of lives
- Significant others hold clear and realistic expectations for the students

Introduction to the Use of Effective Social Support Systems

Success Attribute Covered	Use of Effective Social Support Systems
Familiarity with Success Attributes	Introductory lesson
Suggested Grade Level	Grades 3 to 12
Objective(s)	To define *social support systems*, and identify related concepts
Materials Needed	Worksheet for each student Pens and pencils Chalkboard or display board for teacher notes
Approximate Time	50 minutes

Directions to Implement the Activity	Describe why using effective support systems is included in the Success Attributes (see the Introduction to this book; ask students to complete the worksheet as the following are discussed")
	
	Define:
	
	    Effective
	    Support systems
	    Significant others
	
	Clarify that support systems are place or role dependent (family, friends, people at school support in different ways)
	
	Might include a discussion about how support systems change as people grow up
	
	Describe support systems as a team of people who can help them
	
	Might wish to expand discussion to include the Internet
	
	Ask students to list either roles or names about "who is on their team" as a part of students' support systems

Suggested Modifications	Help with writing assignment Vocabulary discussion might need selection
Caveats Regarding Possible Sensitivity of Topic	Discussion of family may be sensitive to some students May not want students to identify specific people, but rather roles that provide support

Introduction to the Use of Effective Social Support Systems

Directions: Follow the teacher's directions to fill in the blanks below.

1. Write the definition of the following terms in your own words:

   a. *Effective*

   _____

   _____

   b. *Support systems*

   _____

   _____

   c. *Significant others*

   _____

   _____

2. List your possible support systems in five years.

   _____

   _____

3. Who is "on your team" now?

   _____

   _____

Friendship Rating Scale

Success Attribute Covered	Social Support Systems
Familiarity with Success Attributes	Introductory lesson
Suggested Grade Level	Grades 1 to 12
Objective(s)	To hold clear and realistic expectations of self and others
Materials Needed	Worksheet for each student Pens and pencils Ruler to track across lines
Approximate Time	30 minutes Option: may want to spend another 15 minutes presenting the group results of the scale
Directions to Implement the Activity	Ask group to define *friend, friendship,* and *support systems* Discuss the concept of best friend, how friends change over time Introduce rating scale so that the class can think about what is important in friendships Check for understanding of how to complete worksheet May want to provide the option of completing the worksheet independently or reading the prompts to the group one at a time Once worksheets are complete, ask group if there are other attributes or characteristics they consider when they think about friends or themselves that are important for support systems From volunteers, ask which categories on the list were important and which not so important for friendships, and why; as the students review their responses to their evaluation of themselves as a friend, ask them to think about an area where they could improve If the class is interested, the teacher might tally the responses (find the mean, median, mode, if feasible) for students' responses Ask students to draw some conclusions about the survey and friendships from the group responses
Suggested Modifications	Help may be needed to read and understand rating system
Caveats Regarding Possible Sensitivity of Topic	Student may be unable to identify a best friend; in this case, focus on what the student would like in a best friend

Student may be unwilling or be unable to see self as a friend

If the identified best friend is in the class and gets a low rating, feelings might be hurt. The teacher might need to counsel or clarify with both students

May need to emphasize the general nature of best friend and talk about friends as a group

---

Friendship Rating Scale

Directions: Circle one number on the scale that best describes your assessment of the qualities listed for your best friend and you, as a friend. Circling 1 means the worst; 5 means the best; circling 2, 3, or 4 is something in between the two.

My best friend is:

	Worst				Best
Fun to be with, good sense of humor	1	2	3	4	5
Honest	1	2	3	4	5
Sympathetic	1	2	3	4	5
Interested in same activities	1	2	3	4	5
Good at getting over arguments	1	2	3	4	5
Good at sharing	1	2	3	4	5
Supportive	1	2	3	4	5
Helpful	1	2	3	4	5
Not too bossy	1	2	3	4	5
Never gossips about me	1	2	3	4	5

As a friend, I am:

	Worst				Best
Fun to be with, good sense of humor	1	2	3	4	5
Honest	1	2	3	4	5
Sympathetic	1	2	3	4	5
Interested in same activities	1	2	3	4	5
Good at getting over arguments	1	2	3	4	5
Good at sharing	1	2	3	4	5
Supportive	1	2	3	4	5
Helpful	1	2	3	4	5
Not too bossy	1	2	3	4	5
Never willing to gossip about my friend	1	2	3	4	5

Who You Gonna Call?

Success Attribute Covered	Support Systems
Familiarity with Success Attributes	Intermediate lesson
Suggested Grade Level	Grades 4 to 8
Objective(s)	To develop strategies for asking for help
Materials Needed	Worksheet for each student Poster paper Chalkboard Pens and pencils
Approximate Time	30 minutes
Directions to Implement the Activity	Review concepts behind using support systems from previous lessons Select one or two of the scenarios from the worksheet for whole group discussion Ask students to complete worksheet independently or as assigned in small groups Close discussion by asking students to discuss the questions at the end, or if time permits during the following days, ask students to write responses to questions 9 and 10 Emphasize that situations can be small (pencil borrowing) or take on much larger proportions (talking to a friend in need)
Suggested Modifications	Reduce number of scenarios Allow alternatives to writing (addressing scenarios with whole paragraphs, simple sentences, phrases, pictures, or drawings)
Caveats Regarding Possible Sensitivity of Topic	Eliminate subjects that might be too emotional or frightening to address in a group, or be prepared to spend additional individual time with follow-up for specific students

Who You Gonna Call?

Directions: Write your answer to each of the questions below.

1. A friend snubs you.

   Who you gonna call? _____

   Why? _____

2. You get chicken pox.

   Who you gonna call? _____

   Why? _____

3. You have a fight with your best friend.

   Who you gonna call? _____

   Why? _____

4. You fail a test.

   Who you gonna call? _____

   Why? _____

5. You miss the school bus.

   Who you gonna call? _____

   Why? _____

6. You get grounded.

   Who you gonna call? _____

   Why? _____

7. You drop all your books.

   Who you gonna call? _____

   Why? _____

8. Your parents' arguing upsets you.

   Who you gonna call? _____

   Why? _____

9. Describe a situation where you could have or did ask for help.

   _____

   _____

   Who helped, or could have?

   _____

   _____

10. Think of a time when you helped someone or could have.

    _____

    _____

    How did you feel about being a helper, or not being a helper?

    _____

    _____

Strength in Numbers

Success Attribute Covered	Support Systems
Familiarity with Success Attributes	Intermediate lesson
Suggested Grade Level	Grades 3 to 12
Objective(s)	To seek support and attract or draw support from others
Materials Needed	Worksheet for each student Pens and pencils
Approximate Time	30 minutes

Directions to Implement the Activity	Explain or ask for student input to explain the expression, "There is strength in numbers"
	
	Check for group understanding of the expression and relate to support systems
	
	Have the group brainstorm possible solutions (sensible and unrealistic) to a situation that requires some problem solving:
	
	    Students should be able to solve the situation easily. *Example*: running an errand for a parent or wanting to play video games instead of doing homework
	    A more involved idea: what are some things a person could do if that person got lost at an amusement park
	
	Once students have the idea:
	
	    Introduce the worksheet
	    Organize how students will move through the activities, clarifying where they will move once they work individually and in small groups
	    Ensure that the time limit for each is clear and short
	    Perhaps use a signal to indicate when the students must move
	
	When both scenarios are complete, return to the concept that there is strength in numbers, and review how helping each other and asking for help when needed are important to success

Suggested Modifications	More examples of age-appropriate problems might be needed so students are familiar with the concept prior to working on the worksheet:
	
	    Younger students might focus on a school-related problem (for example, trash on playground, navigating the hallways)
	    Older students might focus on a situation in the community (for example, driving or finding a job)

Students may need help with writing or communicating specifics for the scenarios

Grouping students who support one another might help move this activity along; however, if the intent is to challenge specific students to work cooperatively, this might be an activity to do prior to attempting one that involves more commitment

Once both the modeling and the worksheet are completed, students might design scenarios to use in later classes or with another class

Caveats Regarding Possible Sensitivity of Topic	Students will have various life experiences related to each of the scenarios
	Some scenarios may directly relate to a student's life and cause an unintended reaction, so monitoring the groups as brainstorming continues will be essential
	A student's language skills may hinder or help the group problem-solving process

Strength in Numbers

Directions: Write your answer to each of the questions below. At first you will answer by yourself. Then you and other students will write an answer together.

1. Now here's a problem. You are by yourself, and you hear your dog whimpering and realize he is stuck under your house. What should you do?
   Think of as many solutions as you can (for example, "Call his name over and over"), and write them on the lines under the word "Alone."
   Alone

   _____

   _____

   _____

   Now partner up with someone, and compare lists. Add solutions you didn't have before.
   With one or two other students

   _____

   _____

   _____

2. Your school assignment is to work with two other students on a math project. What will you say and do to get the job done?
   Alone

   _____

   _____

   _____

   With one or two other students

   _____

   _____

   _____

"And Seldom Is Heard . . . ": Discouraging Words or Deeds

Success Attribute Covered	Support Systems, Self-Awareness, Emotional Coping Strategies
Familiarity with Success Attributes	Advanced lesson
Suggested Grade Level	Grades 3 to 12
Objective(s)	To recognize "triggers" when help is needed
Materials Needed	Worksheet for each student Pens and pencils Overhead of worksheet
Approximate Time	50 minutes

Directions to Implement the Activity	Introduce the idea that comments, nonverbal behavior, and actions of others and ourselves can have an impact on group or individual feelings:
	
	    Successful people find people who offer positive supports, and learn how to offer positive support to others
	    To recognize that situations can be viewed from several perspectives and that there may be more than one way to respond to a situation is essential for success
	
	Describe one or two situations (at least one negative) where the behaviors of others had an impact on the feelings of the group:
	
	    If there are class rules directly related to this (for instance, respect each other), the students may work more quickly through the scenario
	    For example, a student laughs at another student's performance in the play (or at a student who fell or had a minor accident)
	
	With the group, write a response to each of the prompts on the overhead
	
	Divide group into pairs or other small group arrangements
	
	Ask groups to complete another set of prompts
	
	Set clear time limits for completion
	
	When the groups are finished, ask one person from each group to report on one at least the final prompt: "Better Choices"

Indicate commonalities among responses:

> May want to post the ''Better Choices'' for future reference
> Once the activity is completed, students might have suggestions about topics and scenarios for another class to use

Reinforce concepts from beginning of class

Suggested Modifications	Groups should be designated so that someone in each group can record the answer
	If the teacher acts as recorder, explain how he or she should be contacted once the group has an answer to record
Caveats Regarding Possible Sensitivity of Topic	Teacher or students might inadvertently (or not) identify an extremely sensitive topic
	A possible alternative to group work is to have students complete a response independently after teacher modeling and class discussion
	Teacher should move throughout the room during small group discussion to monitor possible hot topics
	Clear guidelines about the use of unacceptable language must be in place prior to beginning the discussion

"And Seldom Is Heard . . . ": Discouraging Words or Deeds

Directions: Write a summary of your group's answer to each question below.

1. Write a summary of a discouraging situation:

   _____

   _____

2. How you would feel:

   _____

   _____

3. How the other person would probably feel:

   _____

   _____

4. Better choices are:

   _____

   _____

Imagine Me, Imagine You

Success Attribute Covered	Support Systems, Self-Awareness
Familiarity with Success Attributes	Intermediate lesson
Suggested Grade Level	Grades 4 to 12
Objective(s)	To learn to accept feedback and trust in others
Materials Needed	Worksheet for each student
	Pens and pencils
	Display board for terms, if needed
Approximate Time	45 minutes
Directions to Implement the Activity	Discuss the importance of accepting feedback from others; acknowledging that opinions are valid; trusting each other
	Review what physical, personality, and social traits are
	Record list, and check for understanding of group
	Partner students, and ask that first three sections of worksheet be completed independently (state time limits, if needed)
	Ask students to compare responses through discussion, and write answers for questions 4 and 5
	Students may complete final section independently
	As a class, have volunteers provide comments about the activity, relating responses to concepts at beginning of class
Suggested Modifications	Have a list of traits available for students
	May want to use this activity after a science activity, where physical traits were discussed
	Assistance with vocabulary, spelling
Caveats Regarding Possible Sensitivity of Topic	Careful pairing of students is essential to the success of this activity
	Consider this activity after knowing the students well

Imagine Me, Imagine You

1. What do you see in yourself? List your traits.
   Physical traits

   _____

   _____

   Personality traits

   _____

   _____

   Social traits

   _____

   _____

2. What docs your partner scc in you? List what you *think* the partner sees.
   Physical traits

   _____

   _____

   Personality traits

   _____

   _____

   Social traits

   _____

   _____

3. What do you see in your partner?
   Physical traits

   _____

   _____

   Personality traits

   _____

   _____

Social traits

_____

_____

4. Find out if you agree. Read each other's papers.
   Similarities

   _____

   _____

   Differences

   _____

   _____

5. One way the two of you could support each other:

   _____

   _____

What's New?

Success Attribute Covered	Support Systems, Self-Awareness
Familiarity with Success Attributes	Intermediate lesson
Suggested Grade Level	Grades 1 to 12
Objective(s)	To recognize and accept talents along with limitations
Materials Needed	Worksheet for each student Pens and pencils
Approximate Time	30 minutes (10 minutes per interview and 5 minutes each for introduction and closure)
Directions to Implement the Activity	Explain that in order to use support systems effectively, a person needs to know the people in his or her group of support Students may brainstorm reasons that they should know each other well: To support one another To practice getting to know someone else To know whom to go to for help Assign students to pairs and explain the following three parts and vocabulary in the interview, and time limit for each: 1. One student interviews the other and writes the responses on the paper 2. Roles are reversed: the interviewer records the other's responses 3. Students look at responses for similarities and differences When all steps are finished, ask for volunteers to share their findings of what surprised them about the interviews Highlight one or two statements that reinforce using support systems
Suggested Modifications	Students may need assistance recording the answers Older students may need encouragement to elaborate on questions that appear to be basic
Caveats Regarding Possible Sensitivity of Topic	Students might be paired with an individual who is reluctant to share

What's New?

Directions: Partner up with the assigned person. Interview this person as if you are a newscaster about what he or she does creatively (art or music, for example), physically (health, sports, appearance, something else), and socially (friends, organizations).Some examples are underlined on the worksheet.

I interviewed _____ first.

Next _____ interviewed me.

Art, Music, Drama

I know you like to <u>draw</u> _____ and <u>make jewelry</u>

And you are good at <u>photography</u>

When did you begin? _____

So, creatively speaking, what have you done lately? _____

Sports, Health, Exercise, Diet, Appearance

I know you are good at <u>picking out nice clothes</u>

_____

and _____

When did you begin? _____

So, physically speaking, what have you been doing lately?

_____

_____

Friends, Groups

I know you are friends with

_____

and when it comes to friends, you are good at

_____

_____

So what's new with friends or groups you belong to? _____

Is there anything else new in your life?

_____

_____

Now trade places, and have your partner ask you the questions. Tell him or her your answers, and he or she will write them on HIS or HER paper.

_____

_____

Getting to Know You

Success Attribute Covered	Social Support Systems, Self-Awareness
Familiarity with Success Attributes	Intermediate lesson
Suggested Grade Level	Grades 2 to 6
Objective(s)	To learn to accept help, give help, and develop trust in others
Materials Needed	Worksheet for each student
	Pencils and pens for each student
	Display board
Approximate Time	10 minutes of introduction
	10 minutes per interview
	Total of 30 minutes
Directions to Implement the Activity	Introduce support systems: asking someone for help
	Introduce self-awareness: knowing who you are, your strengths and weaknesses
	Begin by talking about talk shows:
	Way to get to know individuals
	Define host as the person asking and listening, celebrity as responder
	Introduce questions, and define boundaries
	Make answers funny, but real and honest
	Host can or cannot ask follow-up questions
	Make sure students understand that when they are the host, they record the celebrity's response
	Instruct the group in how much time is involved
	Students are allowed to select partners
	Student pairs should conduct the interviews, changing roles midpoint through the allotted time
	Ask students which role they like better, and collect suggestions how the roles might be better defined next time
	Ask students if they learned more about themselves or their partner
	Select two or three terms related to support systems and self-awareness, and draw relationship between students' feedback and concepts

Suggested Modifications	Students may need help recording their answers
	Although the activity suggests that students select their own partner, be cautious about pairing students—because some students may share more with others
	Students may need clarity about the concepts within the questions
Caveats Regarding Possible Sensitivity of Topic	Once pairing and veracity are considered, students should be willing to participate readily

Getting to Know You

Interviewer's Name: _____
Date: _____
"Celebrity's" Name: _____

Choose a partner. Decide who will be the talk show host and who will be the celebrity (you will switch roles later). The host will write the answers on his or her worksheet. Then the host asks the celebrity the following questions.

"Tell me three interesting things about yourself."

_____

_____

_____

"Tell me about your talents."

_____

_____

"What would you change about yourself?"

_____

_____

"What are your hopes for the future?"

_____

_____

When you finish, switch roles and repeat the questions.

Human Helpers: Accommodations for School, Work, and Life

Success Attribute Covered	Social Support Systems, Self-Awareness, Proactivity, Emotional Coping Strategies
Familiarity with Success Attributes	Advanced lesson
Suggested Grade Level	Grades 3 to 12
Objective(s)	To practice maintaining contact with significant others
Materials Needed	Worksheets for each student Pens and pencils Overhead transparency of worksheet	If available, examples of assistive technology equipment that are listed on worksheet
Approximate Time	40 minutes
Directions to Implement the Activity	Introduce the word *accommodations:* Accommodations can be written on an Individual Educational Plan, but can also be people who help Integrate some of the related Succcss Attributes' vocabulary to accommodations (knowing what is available, understanding strengths and weaknesses, comprehending what is realistic): Learning to ask for help and trusting others With overhead of worksheet within view, model how to complete worksheet, demonstrating, if possible, or defining specific accommodations listed Monitor students as they complete their own worksheet independently Have volunteers give feedback on their results: May want to list or role-play ideas about asking for help
Suggested Modifications	Students may need assistance with reading the list: Teacher may need to read list to the group May want to group students to complete any or all of the worksheets, especially "Getting What You Need from Helpers" Divide the worksheets into sections, and focus on one section per day, taking a week to complete the lesson
Caveats Regarding Possible Sensitivity of Topic	Some students (and their parents) have various levels of awareness and acceptance of disabilities For students where accommodations are particularly sensitive, this may need to be an independent or one-on-one time with the teacher

Human Helpers: Accommodations for School, Work, and Life

Directions: In each category, check the boxes for the helpers you have used.

Helping Professionals Social Network

☐ teachers
☐ tutors
☐ proofreaders
☐ readers
☐ note takers
☐ transcribers

☐ family
☐ friends
☐ coworkers
☐ fellow students
☐ study group members

Giving Feedback to Helpers

Professional Helpers

☐ tactful requests not to censor
☐ please and thank you
☐ payment
☐ showing appreciation
☐ compliments
☐ gifts
☐ exchange of services
☐ other _____

Family and Friends

☐ tactful requests not to censor
☐ please and thank you
☐ showing appreciation
☐ compliments
☐ gifts
☐ exchange of services
☐ other _____

Getting What You Need From Helpers

Directions: Write an answer to each of the four questions below.

Readers

What you want: reader reads exact words on the page

What you may get: reader substituting "baby" words for difficult vocabulary

How would you ask for it? _____

_____

Tutors

What you want: to be taught the lesson

What you may get: "teaching" by doing the work for you

How would you ask for it? _____

_____

Transcribers

What you want: writing down exactly what you say

What you may get: "proofreading/grammar checking," "correcting" content, criticism

How would you ask for it? _____

_____

Any Other Helper

What you want: assistance with what you need from the helper

What you may get: the answer instead of a hint

How would you ask for it? _____

_____

Delightful Disclosure

Success Attribute Covered	Support Systems, Goal Setting
Familiarity with Success Attributes	Intermediate lesson
Suggested Grade Level	Grades 1 to 12
Objective(s)	To receive support, guidance, and encouragement from significant others
Materials Needed	Worksheet for each student Pens and pencils
Approximate Time	10 minutes
Directions to Implement the Activity	Once a predetermined goal is reached, complete the worksheet Ask a significant other (appropriate for the goal, if possible) to award the student the completed award Give student the option to display the acknowledgment in class, in a folder, or some other way
Suggested Modifications	Teacher should monitor to ensure that all students receive an award for some accomplishment within a realistic time frame Establishing realistic, timely goals for each student may be challenging
Caveats Regarding Possible Sensitivity of Topic	Sensitivity to a student's reaction to public recognition Acknowledgment may need to be done in private

Delightful Disclosure

Name: _____

Date: _____

I am delighted to disclose that _____ *has learned to* _____

_____

We are tickled pink!

Students with strong emotional coping skills:

- Acknowledge that their learning disabilities creates significant stress in their lives
- Key components of their coping strategies are:
  - Recognizing what situations trigger stress
  - Seeking help and support
- Other coping mechanisms they use are:
  - Maintaining good peer relationships
  - Keeping socially active
  - Having a positive, hopeful outlook in the face of difficulty

Introduction to Emotional Coping Strategies

Success Attribute Covered	Emotional Coping Strategies
Familiarity with Success Attributes	Introductory lesson
Suggested Grade Level	Grades 3 to 12
Objective(s)	Define emotional coping strategies and identify related concepts
Materials Needed	Worksheet for each student Pencils and pens Chalkboard or display board for teacher notes
Approximate Time	50 minutes
Directions to Implement the Activity	Describe why emotional strategies are included in the Success Attributes Define the following (ask students to note their comments on their worksheets): *Stress* *Frustration* *Triggers* *Warning signs* *Physical symptoms* *Nonverbal signals* *Coping* *Strategies* Might need to list feelings or kinds of emotions and discuss why emotions can be problematic Ask the group to discuss why peers or other people might help with feelings
Suggested Modifications	Understanding terms might be difficult Assistance with writing
Caveats Regarding Possible Sensitivity of Topic	Working in groups might be problematic if students react strongly to the topic Follow up with specific students might be needed to clarify that everyone has emotions and needs strategies, but all are different

The Six Success Factors for Children with Learning Disabilities

Name: _____   Date: _____

Introduction to Emotional Coping Strategies

Directions: Follow the teacher's directions for filling in the blanks.

1. Write why it is important to know emotional coping strategies.

   _____

2. Write the definition of the following terms in your own words:

   a. *Stress*

   _____

   b. *Frustration*

   _____

   c. *Triggers*

   _____

   d. *Warning signs*

   _____

   e. *Physical symptoms*

   _____

   f. *Nonverbal signals*

   _____

   g. *Coping*

   _____

   h. *Strategies*

   _____

3. Write one sentence to tell why peers or other people might help with feelings.

   _____

Emotional Coping Strategies   **145**

Group Roles

Success Attribute Covered	**Emotional Coping Strategies**
Familiarity with Success Attributes	Introductory lesson
Suggested Grade Level	Grades 1 to 12
Objective(s)	To develop an awareness of various emotional reactions and how these reactions affect behavior
Materials Needed	Worksheet for each student Overhead projector Transparency of group roles (or any classroom display of same information); may want each student to have index card identifying and describing his or her role
Approximate Time	30 minutes
Directions to Implement the Activity	Review concepts related to emotional coping strategies and note objective of lesson Ask class to pay close attention to description of activity so they can readily participate in follow-up activity As roles are revealed, define or describe each on the overhead transparency Assign each student (randomly or deliberately) a role within the group (they may need additional help understanding play acting and role playing) Explain that the group is going to discuss where to go on a field trip (if an actual field trip is possible, student involvement may increase) and that each student should participate in the discussion based on the role assigned Lead the group into a discussion of the field trip, and monitor their ability to stay within their assigned roles; May need to ask pointed questions to specific students to encourage discussion (for instance, a student who is quiet and is supposed to play the role of a blocker may not be effective without some prompting or practice) End discussion by indicating clearly to the students that the role playing has stopped Ask for feedback from the group, referencing specific statements made by group members Check that all participants (individually and small groups) are clear that statements were not taken personally

Students should complete the questionnaire independently; check for understanding of reality and the situation, as presented:

With what role they most identified, compatible or incompatible

With what role they felt comfortable (compatible) or uncomfortable (incompatible)

List three strategies for dealing with a group role that was most difficult

Suggested Modifications	Teacher may want each student to have either a worksheet revealing all of the roles or put titles and definitions on index cards, so each student understands his or her specific role
	If a group of students can work independently with minimal teacher involvement, divide students into specific groups to practice a variety of roles
	If time allows, rotate students through a variety of roles, and ask for written or oral reflection about how they felt when the roles shifted
	For younger students, rename the roles:
	For instance, "Peacemaker" might be "Sheriff Woody" or some other cartoon or TV character
	Students may have suggestions about other roles to add to the list, or roles may need to be abbreviated (three instead of seven)
Caveats Regarding Possible Sensitivity of Topic	Students may have difficulty distinguishing between play acting and reality or students may use the role playing to bully another student indirectly
	Roles may need to be revised for specific group needs (only positive, friendly, supportive roles may be assigned initially, for instance)

Group Roles

The following example is for a group that is deciding on music for a party.

Role	What They Do	What They May Say
Starter	Helps start discussion	"We have to decide which music we want."
	Brings up new ideas	"I think we should look at this."
Reviewer	Brings group up to date	"It sounds like we're making progress."
	Points out differences of opinion	"Most of us want rock music, but some want rap music."
Peacemaker	Settles differences and arguments	"Let's find a way to combine both ideas."
	Relieves tension, sometimes by cracking jokes	"That reminds me of a story."
Follower	Goes along with everyone else	"I don't care. Let's do whatever the rest of you think."
Clown	Spends most of the time fooling around	"How about playing video games?"
Blocker	Always disagrees with the group	"You're all wrong."
Dictator	Tries to control the group; bosses people around	"Now you listen to me." "This is the only way to do it."

Group Roles: Questionnaire

Directions: Think about role that you played. Then answer the questions below independently.

1. What role did you most identify yourself with?

   _____

2. What group role did you feel the most comfortable or compatible with? Why?

   _____

   _____

3. What group role did you feel the least comfortable or compatible with?

_____

4. List three strategies for dealing with a group role that you are not compatible with.

a. _____

b. _____

c. _____

A Mile in Your Shoes

Success Attribute Covered	Emotional Coping Strategies
Familiarity with Success Attributes	Intermediate lesson
Suggested Grade Level	Grades 1 to 12
Objective(s)	To recognize situations that "trigger" stress
Materials Needed	Worksheet for each student Pens and pencils Chalkboard
Approximate Time	1 hour

Directions to Implement the Activity	Introduce the adages, "You don't know a person until you walk a mile in their shoes," and "Put yourself in my shoes"
	
	Ask students if they are up to the challenge of thinking about how someone else might feel
	
	Model through this example: imagine life as the youngest child in a family of five (or some large number relative to your community):
	
	    Record students' responses to what would be great and not so great about being the youngest child
	
	Ask students to list other kinds of people whose feelings they would like to consider:
	
	    TV, movie, or book characters
	    Members of the community (clerks in stores, owners of business, government officials)
	    Older or younger students in this or another school
	
	Assign one character or person from the list to each of the students
	
	Ask students to complete the worksheet
	
	When students have completed individual worksheets, pair them to compare answers
	
	If time allows, ask the entire group for to share responses; identify key triggers of stress

Suggested Modifications	Assistance with writing Some prompting with clarification questions might be needed for students with language processing difficulties
Caveats Regarding Possible Sensitivity of Topic	Limit selection of persons so conversation stays focused Monitor nonverbal responses of students for sensitive issues

A Mile in Your Shoes

Directions: Think about a character or person from the list you brainstormed in class. That person is _____.

Now describe how you imagine a typical day in your profile person's life, through his or her eyes. How does this person feel . . .

Getting up in the morning? _____

Getting on the bus? _____

Getting a bad grade? _____

Interacting with others? _____

Sitting down to do homework? _____

What words would this person use to describe himself or herself? _____

More comments:

_____

_____

First Steps

Success Attribute Covered	Emotional Coping Strategies, Support Systems
Familiarity with Success Attributes	Introductory lesson
Suggested Grade Level	Grades 1 to 12
Objective(s)	To develop coping mechanisms to develop and maintain good peer relationships
Materials Needed	Worksheet for each student Pens and pencils Ruler for tracking survey items Overhead of worksheet
Approximate Time	30 minutes to introduce 30 minutes a week later to discuss results
Directions to Implement the Activity	Introduce the concept that friends can help cope with stress and give new ideas when there is a problem Address the notion that some people have best friends and some do not at different times Discuss that new friends are made when someone makes a first move Highlight that sometimes "first moves" may result in friendships, but at other times may not, and that to try is important Students may volunteer times when an initial "move" did or did not result in a friendship Distribute worksheet, and ask students to read all (or part of) it Demonstrate how students should mark each item, noting the day and the individual Students may volunteer to role-play one or two of the "friendly first steps" Ask students to independently select at least five first steps to try during the week with different classmates who may not be good friends of the individual At the end of the week, compile the attempts of the group, noting similarities and differences Discuss a plan for continuing the exercise, not the pros and cons of the activity Review why friends are important to emotional coping strategies

Suggested Modifications	Have multiple examples (pictures, faces, stories) to explain friendly first steps
	Read worksheet to students; reduce number of options for students
	Check for understanding by asking students to write, explain, or draw possible social interactions
	Have students read list independently or as a whole group
Caveats Regarding Possible Sensitivity of Topic	Monitor students' reactions to some other students' responses that may be unrealistic
	Clarify possible roadblocks for individual students, like tone of voice and timing of comments

First Steps

List your friends: _____

Date: _____

Directions: After reading the list, check at least five of the "First Steps." For each of the checked steps, write the day or date you will try to do it, and write the name of the person you will select for the step.

Friendly First Steps	Day	Who
Smile at a classmate	Monday	Mary
Make a play date with a classmate	_____	_____
Say hello first to someone	Thursday	Susie
Eat lunch with a classmate	_____	_____
Talk to a classmate you don't know well	_____	_____
Make something for a classmate	_____	_____
Say something nice to a classmate	_____	_____
Help a classmate clean up	_____	_____
Help someone with schoolwork	_____	_____
Play with a classmate at recess	Tuesday	Robin
Let a classmate go first in a game	_____	_____
Teach a classmate how to do something fun	_____	_____
Start a conversation with a classmate	_____	_____
Give a classmate a compliment	_____	_____
Ask a classmate a question about himself or herself	_____	_____
Find out a classmate's favorite movie, and talk about it	_____	_____
Play (initiate) a game with a classmate	_____	_____
Walk home or to the bus with a classmate	_____	_____
Find out a classmate's hobbies	_____	_____
Ask a classmate about his or her pets	_____	_____
Find out what a classmate wants for a birthday present	_____	_____
Lend a classmate a pencil, pen, or paper or something else	_____	_____

Share your dessert with a classmate   _____   _____

Write a secret note to someone with a compliment in it   _____   _____

Send an e-mail to a classmate   _____   _____

Call a classmate on the phone   _____   _____

Call a classmate who was out sick   _____   _____

_____   _____   _____

_____   _____   _____

At the end of the week, compare your list of friends to last week.

Have you made any friends not on your earlier list?_____

What did you do as a first step?_____

What Helps?

Success Attribute Covered	Emotional Coping Strategies, Self-Awareness
Familiarity with Success Attributes	Advanced lesson
Suggested Grade Level	Grades 1 to 12
Objective(s)	To learn to recognize when outside support or help is needed
Materials Needed	Worksheet for each student Pens and pencils Overhead or chalkboard to record ideas for first question
Approximate Time	50 minutes
Directions to Implement the Activity	Have the group brainstorm emotions, and record them on the chalkboard Highlight emotions that students will focus on from worksheet (afraid, sad, happy) Distribute the "afraid" worksheet: As a class, gather responses to each question Students should complete each question with you After the "afraid" worksheet is completed, students should independently complete subsequent worksheets Once all worksheets are complete, volunteers will share specific portions of their answers; noting both the intensity of the emotion and the strategy to cope

Suggested Modifications	Alternatives to writing:
	    In small groups, students could create a skit demonstrating an example
	    Students could draw a picture and then explain
	    Might find or have previously read literature where the character demonstrates one or more of the emotions

Caveats Regarding Possible Sensitivity of Topic	Initially, explain how the confidentiality of answers will be ensured:
	    How to indicate to the teacher if a private discussion is needed
	    How to indicate if a response may be shared by highlight or folded paper
	
	Make sure to ask for volunteers for any class sharing
	
	If students are uncomfortable sharing their own experiences, all students may create all responses, or find a character from books or another media that demonstrates the emotions listed

What Helps?

Remember the last time you were *afraid*.

What happened?

_____

_____

What did you do?

_____

_____

What did you want to happen?

_____

_____

What or who helped?

_____

_____

What were the actual consequences of what you did or didn't do?

_____

_____

What Helps?

Remember the last time you were *sad*.

What happened?

_____

_____

What did you do?

_____

_____

What did you want to happen?

_____

_____

What or who helped?

_____

_____

What were the actual consequences of what you did or didn't do?

_____

_____

What Helps?

Have you ever been happy and it got you into trouble?

What happened?

_____

_____

What did you do?

_____

_____

What did you want to happen?

_____

_____

What or who helped?

_____

_____

What were the actual consequences of what you did or didn't do?

_____

_____

How Does It Feel?

Success Attribute Covered	Emotional Coping Strategies, Self-Awareness
Familiarity with Success Attributes	Introductory lesson May want to pair with "What Helps?"
Suggested Grade Level	Grades 4 to 12
Objective(s)	To develop an understanding of the factors that affect psychological health
Materials Needed	Worksheet for each student Pens and pencils
Approximate Time	30 minutes
Directions to Implement the Activity	Review concepts of emotions, reactions, feelings, and self-awareness
	Associate that one's emotions are usually a reaction to an event and that being aware of one's feelings and what causes those feelings is important
	Emotions are also linked to physical well-being:
	When emotions are positive, a person feels better physically than when emotions are negative Awareness of emotions, feelings, and reactions is an important first step in identifying strategies to help feel and act better
	Another important concept is for students to realize that everyone has different reactions and strategies for dealing with them
	Sharing strategies helps to broaden strategies available, and other people might select a different strategy under similar circumstances
	Ask students to complete the worksheet independently
	Monitor students for those who are struggling with vocabulary
	When all worksheets are complete, ask volunteers to share their findings
	Teacher may want to elaborate on similarities and differences among the responses
	Teacher should reinforce and list the importance of a variety of strategies to cope with feelings
	As follow-up, pairs, small groups, or the entire class may develop a poster or pamphlet representing a collection of the strategies they created

The Six Success Factors for Children with Learning Disabilities

Suggested Modifications	For younger children, the teacher might want to have a diagram of the human body to show connection between emotional and physical reactions; list physical reactions
	Encourage movement by asking students to tense the part of their body being discussed or acting out an emotion using a specific body part (for instance, how their face looks when they are afraid)
	May need to list possible words associated with specific emotions (*tense, relaxed, tight, nervous, shaking*)
Caveats Regarding Possible Sensitivity of Topic	Teacher should monitor reactions of students as they are completing or discussing worksheets

How Does It Feel?

Directions: Put a word on the blank that describes how you feel when afraid, angry, sad, or happy.

	Afraid (fear)	**Angry** (anger)	**Sad** (depressed)	**Happy** (love)
Stomach	_____	_____	_____	_____
Heart	_____	_____	_____	_____
Chest	_____	_____	_____	_____
Face	_____	_____	_____	_____
Neck	_____	_____	_____	_____
What do you want to do when you are feeling this way?	_____	_____	_____	_____
Whom do you like being with when you are feeling this way ?	_____	_____	_____	_____

Do Something!

Success Attribute Covered	Emotional Coping Strategies, Proactivity
Familiarity with Success Attributes	Advanced lesson
Suggested Grade Level	Grades 1 to 12
Objective(s)	To develop a repertoire of coping strategies
Materials Needed	Worksheets for each student Pens and pencils Ruler for tracking lines
Approximate Time	30 minutes
Directions to Implement the Activity	Distribute worksheets, and review the vocabulary as a group Have students act out various activities identified on the worksheet, using nonverbal communication (body and facial expressions) Ask students to work independently, checking strategies that they have tried when they were angry As they are completing the checklist, they should add their own new ideas: If they are struggling, they may want to pair with another student to create other strategies Have volunteers share new strategies May want to tally which of the strategies were most and least identified by the group and discuss reasons
Suggested Modifications	Brainstorm new ideas section of the worksheet as a group Read the list to the group, and allow time for students to respond by checking the first column May want to complete one category during one class period
Caveats Regarding Possible Sensitivity of Topic	Consider students' emotional states

Do Something!

Directions: Check the activities you have tried when you are angry. Add other ideas at the bottom of the page.

Do Something Physical

_____ go for a walk

_____ dance

_____ punch something soft

_____ shoot some baskets

_____ breathe deeply ten times

_____ throw something soft

Do Something Fun

_____ watch a favorite video

_____ listen to a favorite song

_____ play a video game

Do Something Soothing

_____ take a bubble bath

_____ meditate

Do Something Social

_____ call a friend

_____ play a game with someone

Do Something Artistic

_____ sing a song

_____ make something

_____ write a poem

_____ act out a scene about situation

_____ write a funny story about it

Do Something Useful

_____ clean something

_____ mow the lawn

_____ change the oil in the car

_____ clean a closet

Do Something Alone

_____ take a time out

_____ scream into a pillow

New Ideas

_____   _____

Name Your Bandages

Success Attribute Covered	Emotional Coping Strategies
Familiarity with Success Attributes	Intermediate lesson
Suggested Grade Level	Grades 1 to 12
Objective(s)	To learn to recognize from whom and when to seek help and support
Materials Needed	Worksheet for each student Pens and pencils Chalkboard or any classroom display
Approximate Time	50 minutes

Directions to Implement the Activity	Explain that emotional hurt can feel the same as physical hurt:
	
	    Feeling sad or angry might feel the same as being cut, scraped, or bruised
	    One can think of getting help with emotional pain is the same as getting a bandage for a physical injury
	
	Distribute the worksheet, and ask students to complete it independently
	
	Ask the group to give examples of emotional injuries that might require a support person bandage
	
	If possible, the group might indicate that some people provide different bandages for different injuries:
	
	    For instance, sometimes a person might listen, and sometimes the same person might give advice or help problem-solve
	
	Ask the group to name people they can call for a "bandage" from their worksheet
	
	List that group on the board

Suggested Modifications	To help with responses, the support and bandage people might be listed in categories like school, community, home Select or have each student select some of the situations listed If pairs of students work together, assign pairs based on compatibility
Caveats Regarding Possible Sensitivity of Topic	If a student lists an unpredictable support person, be cautious in asking why that person might be listed (the student's reason might need confidentiality from the group) Encourage students to list roles, not names of people If students hesitate to clarify their reasoning, respect their hesitation

Name Your Bandages

Situation	Bandage	
Rejection	Who	_____
	Why	_____
Poor grades	Who	_____
	Why	_____
Fighting with your best friend	Who	_____
	Why	_____
Failure to make the team	Who	_____
	Why	_____
Friend with a problem	Who	_____
	Why	_____
Family problems	Who	_____
	Why	_____
Illness	Who	_____
	Why	_____

Help Me Cope

Success Attribute Covered	Emotional Coping Strategies
Familiarity with Success Attributes	Intermediate lesson
Suggested Grade Level	Grades 4 to 12
Objective(s)	To develop strategies for avoiding stress
Materials Needed	Worksheet for each student Pens and pencils Chalkboard (overhead display)
Approximate Time	30 minutes

Directions to Implement the Activity	Discuss common stressors in life; record responses on board
	Weight stressors as low (1), medium (2), and high (3)
	Identify strategies for coping with each identified stressor:
	    Support from people you know
	    Acknowledging those events that you cannot control
	Once group ideas are posted, students should record individual responses (either from the board or elsewhere) on worksheet; encourage other ideas
	Monitor the individual responses
	If time is available (or if realistic), have students volunteer to share their responses in small groups you assign

Suggested Modifications	May want to provide examples that might initiate discussion (taking a test, getting corrected by a teacher) Check for understanding through role playing May want to implement prior to an event that may be stressful to a large number of students (group standardized testing, competitive tournaments)
Caveats Regarding Possible Sensitivity of Topic	May need to limit areas of discussion to global issues State that some issues may need private discussion and ask that students make individual appointments

Help Me Cope

Directions: Fill in the blanks. Use the some of the notes from the class, or respond with your own thoughts that were not discussed.

1. List three times when you felt stress.

_____

_____

_____

2. Describe how you reacted to one or more of those situations.

_____

_____

_____

3. Did your reaction help? If not, what might have been a better choice?

_____

_____

_____

Welcome, Stranger

Success Attribute Covered	**Emotional Support, Proactivity**
Familiarity with Success Attributes	Introductory lesson
Suggested Grade Level	Grades 1 to 12
Objective(s)	To develop strategies for keeping socially active
Materials Needed	Worksheet for each student Pens and pencils
Approximate Time	Brief introduction during class 30 minutes during nonacademic time
Directions to Implement the Activity	Ask for student input about the need to feel welcome in a new situation Brainstorm ideas about what can be said or done to help someone new feel comfortable in school Establish the concept that students react differently to different situations and that is okay Ask if students would like to help welcome a new student to the school For those who volunteer, divide the tasks listed on the worksheet after ensuring that all understand the assignments At the end of the time, ask the volunteers to reflect on the tasks, answer questions on the worksheet, and check for revisions for the next time
Suggested Modifications	Students may be assigned to do parts of this lesson More options may be necessary The more students who are engaged, the more welcome the new person will feel Role-playing this activity, either as a substitute or a preliminary activity, might be needed
Caveats Regarding Possible Sensitivity of Topic	Monitor students to make sure no one is overwhelming the new student by helping too much

Welcome, Stranger

1. Choose one of these get-acquainted tasks:

   a. Sit with the newcomer at lunch and find out about him or her.

   b. Show the new student where the office, nurse, playground, and cafeteria are.

   c. Volunteer to be his or her partner in class for some activity (art, reading group, something else).

   d. Go to recess or break with the student.

   e. Some other activity you think important_____

2. NOW be a good citizen/welcomer. Find out:

   a. The new student's favorite foods _____

   b. The new student's favorite game, sport, or other activity _____

   c. Where the student moved from _____

3. What else did you talk about? _____

   _____

   _____

4. Introduce the new student to one or more of your friends OR invite him or her to be with your group for games, conversation or whatever else you do when you have free time. What happened?

   _____

5. How did you feel after you reached out to a new person?

   _____

   _____

6. Will you do it again? _____ Why or why not?_____

   _____

Appendix A: Resources for Fostering the Success Attributes

Children's Literature

Two book lists are provided in this resource section. The first is of books whose main characters have learning problems. The Frostig research team selected these books as accurately depicting learning difficulties and illustrating one or more Success Attributes within the context of a child struggling with a learning difficulty. The attributes represented in the story are identified at the end of the description of each book. The list is not inclusive, and teachers are encouraged to select their own books as well.

The second list of books has been selected by a distinguished panel of children's authors, librarians, and children's book reviewers. Each book is believed to represent exemplary children's literature and to illustrate one or more Success Attributes within the story. This list of books does not include characters with learning problems.

Ways to Use Books to Foster the Success Attributes

Literature can be used to help children gain self-awareness and solve problems. The use of books with this purpose in mind is called *bibliotherapy*. Bibliotherapy has been suggested as a way to help students with learning disabilities develop problem-solving strategies, know that there are other people with problems similar to theirs, develop insights into their feelings and behaviors, and contribute to their self-concept (Hildreth & Candler, 1992; Forgan, 2002; Sridhar & Vaughn, 2000).

Additional books chosen for this purpose should be well written and have literary merit (Aiex, 1993). Poorly written material will do little to foster interest, provoke thought, or encourage introspection. Teachers need to determine whether individual or group sessions are the most appropriate for their particular situations.

Tu (1999) suggests that literature used to help children cope with problems include the following features:

- Be well written and age appropriate
- Provide language that is familiar to students and is realistic in terms of their life experiences
- Honestly portray the situation and future possibilities for the characters
- Present multidimensional characters experiencing legitimate emotions with whom they can relate
- Offer potential for controversy

- Explore the process of working out problems
- Demonstrate clear channels of communication and responses to children's questions
- Offer situations that generate enthusiasm in the reader

Aiex (1993) offers these guidelines:

- Motivate students with introductory activities.
- Provide time for reading the material.
- Allow "incubation" time.
- Provide follow-up discussion time that will lead students to interpret, apply, analyze, synthesize, and evaluate the information.
- Conduct teacher evaluations and student self-evaluations.

Forgan (2002) has made several suggestions for how to teach problem solving through literature to students with disabilities, including learning disabilities. He recommends the following sequence of activities:

1. *Prereading.* The teacher selects material, activates students' background knowledge, and helps them link their experiences with the book.
2. *Guide reading.* The teacher reads the story out loud and lets students reflect by writing their reactions a literature journals.
3. *Postreading discussion.* Students retell the story and are asked probing questions to ensure they understand it.
4. *Problem solving.* Students develop independent problem-solving strategies.

Hildreth and Candler (1992) proposed a series of questions considered to be effective for using reading materials to help students with learning disabilities better understand themselves and their problems. This list of questions has been adapted specifically for probing the Success Attributes:

- What was the story about?
- Who were the main characters?
- Can you describe them?
- Did any of the characters demonstrate any of the Success Attributes at the beginning of the story?
- Did any of the characters develop the Success Attributes as the story progressed?
- What specific attributes did they have?
- Did some characters have these attributes more than other characters?
- Why do you think this was the case?
- What specific attributes did they learn about?
- How were these attributes developed?
- What circumstances led to the development of these attributes?
- Did the characters get help from anyone in learning these attributes?
- How did the attributes help them?
- Do you think the characters could have solved their problems or been successful without the success attributes?

- Do you think they will use these attributes in other situations? Why or why not?
- How do you think you would have solved the problem?
- Do you think you have the that helped the characters) solve their problem, reach their goal, or achieve success?

Book Lists

Characters with Learning Problems

The Beast in Ms. Rooney's Room, by Patricia Reilly Giff. IL: K-3; RL: 3.2 It's September again. What does it mean for Richard "Beast" Best to be left back? It means being teased by his old friends while stuck facing the same old teacher in the same old classroom. He even has to take a special reading class with "babies" like Emily Arrow and Matthew Jackson. And just like last year, he can't help getting into trouble. But with the help of Mrs. Paris, the reading teacher, Beast starts to enjoy reading and just might find a way to help the second grade win the school banner for best class. *Success Attribute:* Use of Social Support Systems.

The Best Fight, by Anne Schlieper. IL: 3–6; RL: 4.5 Fifth-grader Jamie, who goes to a special class because he has difficulty reading, thinks he's dumb until the school principal helps him realize that he also has many talents. *Success Attributes:* Self-Awareness, Emotional Coping Strategies.

Different Is Not Bad, Different Is the World: A Book About Disabilities, by Sally L. Smith. IL: 3–6; RL: 4.8 A children's book that teaches about disabilities in a positive way. The simple words and colorful illustrations teach empathy and acceptance of differences. *Success Attribute:* Self-Awareness.

Do Bananas Chew Gum? by Jamie Gilson. IL: 3–6; RL: 5.3 Sam Mott acts like a smart aleck to keep from looking dumb. He has made it most of the way through sixth grade barely able to read and write. Now his family has moved again, and none of the kids in his new school has started calling him Dumbhead Sam yet. But how long can Sam keep his problem secret when even the second grader he baby-sits for reads better than he does? *Success Attribute:* Self-Awareness, Use of Social Support Systems.

Dolphin Sky, by G. Rorby. IL: 5–8; RL: 6. Twelve-year-old Buddy, whose dyslexia makes things difficult for her at home and at school, hopes to rescue the dolphins that are being held captive and mistreated at a swamp farm near her home in the Everglades. *Success Attributes:* Proactivity, Emotional Coping Strategies, Use of Social Support Systems

Eli: The Boy Who Hated to Write: Understanding Dysgraphia, by Eli Richards. IL: YA; RL: YA. Throughout the story, Eli describes his feelings about writing and the reactions of his peers and teachers to his dysgraphia. After a significant adventure, Eli and his friends realize that everyone is different, with varying combinations of strengths and weaknesses. Several appendixes include actual stories written by Eli in elementary school and a list of strategies for students with writing problems. An epilogue presents an allegory written by Eli in college. *Success Attribute:* Self-Awareness.

The Flunking of Joshua T. Ba, by Susan Richards Shreve. IL: 3–6; RL: 3.2. Joshua is mortified to discover that he has to repeat third grade. Not only does he have to deal with his own embarrassment, he also has to put up with the taunts of his former classmates. To top it off, his new teacher, Mrs. Goodwin, looks like a tank. But she turns out to be kind and understanding and takes the time to help him. With her help, Joshua makes it through the year and learns something important about himself. *Success Attributes:* Perseverance, Use of Social Support Systems.

The Hard Life of Seymour E. New, by Ann Bixby Herold. IL: 9–12. A third grader with learning difficulties is heartened by a spider he names Seymour, who rebuilds his web as necessary, and by finding out his father has a problem similar to his own *Success Attributes*; Perseverance.

I Know I Can Climb the Mount, by Dale S. Brown. IL: YA; RL: YA. This anthology of fifty-three poems and three short stories shows the experience of a person who takes charge of her own life despite difficulties and challenges. The author, a woman who wrote these poems during her childhood and teenage years, experienced a difference currently called by many names: specific learning disabilities, attention deficit hyperactivity disorder, and dyslexia. She was in a general education class and received virtually no help for the challenges she experienced. *Success Attributes:* Perseverance, Self-Awareness, Proactivity.

I'm Somebody, by Jeanne Gehret. IL: 3–6; RL: 5.3. Twelve-year-old Emily has a younger brother, Ben, who is hyperactive and a slow learner. Her worry about him affects her schoolwork and her peer relationships. Her family tends to be in denial about all of this. Feelings are hidden until her parents seek professional help. They learn that Ben has attention deficit disorder, which is treatable through structuring his behavior and medication. As Ben becomes calmer and more organized and the family engages in activities together, Emily experiences feelings of jealousy, rage, and guilt. What saves her is an inner voice, a dialogue with her frustration and anger and with her protective love for her brother. She is finally able to deal with her ambivalence by recognizing that it is a part of her. *Success Attribute:* Use of Social Support Systems.

Spaceman, by Jane Cutler. IL: 5–8; RL: 5.5. Gary just can't seem to fit in. He doesn't have any friends, his school work is always sloppy, and his teachers endlessly criticize him. To escape, he spaces out. One day Gary accidentally hurts someone and is being sent to a new school for kids with different learning styles. Will Gary finally be able to catch up and fit in, or will he remain the Spaceman forever? *Success Attributes:* Self-Awareness, Use of Social Support Systems.

Thank You, Mr. Falker, by Patricia Polacco. IL: K–4; RL: 4.8. Little Trisha is overjoyed at the thought of starting school and learning how to read. But when she looks at a book, all the letters and numbers get jumbled up. Her classmates make matters worse by calling her Dummy. Only Mr. Falker, a stylish, fun-loving new teacher, recognizes Trisha's incredible artistic ability—and her problem—and takes the time to lead her finally and happily to the magic of reading. This autobiographical story is close to author Patricia Polacco's heart. It is her personal song of thanks to teachers like Mr. Falker who quietly but surely change the lives of the children they teach. *Success Attributes:* Perseverance, Use of Social Support Systems.

Yours Turly, Shirley, by Ann M. Martin. IL: 5–8; RL: 5.3. Shirley, a fourth grader with dyslexia, struggles with her feelings of inferiority as she compares herself to her intellectually gifted older brother and newly adopted Vietnamese sister. *Success Attributes:* Use of Social Support Systems, Perseverance.

General Children's Literature

Books are categorized by success attribute, and each includes an indication of interest level (IL) and reading level (RL); some books are suitable for young adults (YA).

Self-Awareness

After the Rain, by Norma Fox Mazer. IL: YA; RL: 5.3. After discovering her grandfather is dying, fifteen-year-old Rachel gets to know him better than ever before and finds the experience bittersweet.

Bad Case of Stripes, by David Shannon. IL: K–3; RL: 3.5. In order to ensure her popularity, Camilla Cream always does what is expected, until the day arrives when she no longer recognizes herself.

Caddie Woodlawn, by Carol Ryrie Brink. IL: 5–8; RL: 5.3. The adventures of an eleven-year-old tomboy growing up on the Wisconsin frontier in the mid-nineteenth century.

Chrysanthemum, by Kevin Henkes. IL: K-3; RL: 4.2. Chrysanthemum loves her name—until she starts going to school and the other children make fun of it.

Dillon Dillon, by Kate Banks. IL: 3–6; RL: 5.3. During the summer when he turns ten years old, Dillon Dillon learns the surprising story behind his name and develops a relationship with three loons living on the lake near his family's New Hampshire cabin. The loons help him make sense of his life.

Fanny's Dream, by Caralyn Buehner. IL: K-3; RL: 2.8. Fanny Agnes is a sturdy farm girl who dreams of marrying a prince, but when her fairy godmother does not show up, she decides on a local farmer instead.

Grandfather's Journey, by Allan Say. IL: K-3; RL: 4.2. A Japanese American recounts his grandfather's journey to America, which he also later undertakes, and the feelings of being torn by a love for two countries.

Hatchet, by Gary Paulsen. IL: 3–6; RL: 5.9. After a plane crash, thirteen-year-old Brian spends fifty-four days in the Canadian wilderness. Here he learns to survive with only the aid of a hatchet given him by his mother and also to survive his parents' divorce.

Hattie Blue Sky, by Kirby Larson. IL: YA; RL: YA. Sixteen-year-old Hattie Brooks inherits her uncle's homesteading claim in Montana in 1917 and encounters some unexpected problems related to the war in Europe.

Holes, by Louis Sachar. IL: 5–8; RL: 6.5. As further evidence of his family's bad fortune, which they attribute to a curse on a distant relative, Stanley Yelnats is sent to a hellish correctional camp in the Texas desert. However, here he finds his first real friend, a treasure, and a new sense of himself.

House of the Scorpion, by Nancy Farmer. IL: 5–8, YA; RL: 6.3. In a future where humans despise clones, Matt enjoys special status as the young clone of El Patrón, the 142-year-old leader of a corrupt drug empire nestled between Mexico and the United States.

House of Sports, by Marisabina Russo. IL: 3–6; RL: 6.3. Through a series of triumphs and tragedies at home, at school, and on the basketball court, plus time reluctantly spent with his elderly grandmother, twelve-year-old Jim Malone learns that there is a lot more to life than basketball.

Jennifer, Hecate, MacBeth, William McKinley, and Me, Elizabeth, by E. L. Konigsburg. IL: 3–6; RL: 4.7. Two fifth-grade girls, one of whom is the first black child in a middle-income suburb, play at being apprentice witches.

Keeper of the Doves, by Betsy Byars. IL: 3–6; RL: 5.7. In the late 1800s in Kentucky, Amie McBee and her four sisters both fear and torment the reclusive and seemingly sinister Mr. Tominski, but their father continues to provide for his needs.

Leo the Late Bloomer, by Robert Krauss. IL: K-3; RL: 1.7. Leo, a young tiger, finally blooms under the anxious eyes of his parents.

Love, Stargirl, by Jerry Spinelli. IL: 5–8; RL: 4.1. Still moping months after being dumped by her Arizona boyfriend, Leo, fifteen-year-old Stargirl, a home-schooled free spirit, writes "the world's longest letter" to Leo, describing her new life in Pennsylvania.

Love That Dog, by Sharon Creech. IL: 3–6; RL: 4.1. A young student who comes to love poetry through a personal understanding of what different famous poems mean to him surprises himself by writing his own inspired poem.

Mufaro's Beautiful Daughter, by John Steptoe. IL: K-3; RL: 5.2. Mufaro's two beautiful daughters, one bad tempered and the other kind and sweet, go before the king, who is choosing a wife.

My Best Friend, by Mary Ann Rodman. IL: K-3; RL: 6.6. Six-year-old Lily has a best friend all picked out for play group day, but unfortunately, the differences between first graders and second graders are sometimes very large.

Olive's Ocean, by Kevin Henkes. IL: 5–8; RL: 6.6. On a summer visit to her grandmother's cottage by the ocean, twelve-year-old Martha gains perspective on the death of a classmate, her relationship with her grandmother, her feelings for an older boy, and her plans to be a writer.

Stargirl, by Jerry Spinelli. IL: 5–8; RL: 6.1. In this story about the perils of popularity, the courage of nonconformity, and the thrill of first love, an eccentric student named Stargirl changes Mica High School forever.

Surviving the Applewhites, by Stephanie Tolan. IL: 5–8, YA; RL: 5.7. Jake, a budding juvenile delinquent, is sent for home schooling to the arty and eccentric Applewhite family's Creative Academy, where he discovers talents and interests he never knew he had.

Ugly Duckling, by Hans Christian Andersen. IL: K-3; RL: NR. An ugly duckling spends an unhappy year ostracized by the other animals before he grows into a beautiful swan.

Watsons Go to Birmingham—1963, by Christopher Paul Curtis. IL: 5–8; RL: 5.0. The ordinary interactions and everyday routines of the Watsons, an African American family living in Flint, Michigan, drastically change after they visit Grandma in Alabama in the summer of 1963.

Year of Impossible Goodbyes, by Sook Nyul Choi. IL: 5–8; RL: 6.3. A young Korean girl survives the oppressive Japanese and Russian occupation of North Korea during the 1940s, later to escape to freedom in South Korea.

Perseverance

Abel's Island, by William Steig. IL: 3–6; RL: 5.5. Cast away on an uninhabited island, Abel, a very civilized mouse, finds his resourcefulness and endurance tested to the limit as he struggles to survive and return to his home.

Airmail to the Moon, by Tom Birdseye. IL: K-3; RL: 3.9. When the tooth that she was saving for the tooth fairy disappears, Ora Mae sets out to find the thief and send him "airmail to the moon!"

Alabama Moon, by Watt Key. IL: 5–8; RL: 5.3. After the death of his father, ten-year-old Moon Blake is removed from the Alabama forest where he was raised and sent to a boys' home, where, for the first time, he has contact with the outside world and learns about friendship, love, and humanity.

The Alfred Summer, by Jan Slepian. IL: 5–8; RL: 6.1. Four preteen outcasts, two of them with disabilities, learn lessons in courage and perseverance when they join forces to build a boat.

Being Teddy Roosevelt, by Claudia Mills. IL: K-3; RL: 3.8. When he is assigned Teddy Roosevelt as his biography project in school, fourth-grader Riley finds himself inspired by Roosevelt's tenacity and perseverance and resolves to find a way to get what he most wants: a saxophone and music lessons.

Brave Irene, by William Steig. IL: K-3; RL: 3.5. Plucky Irene, a dressmaker's daughter, braves a fierce snowstorm to deliver a new gown to the duchess in time for the ball.

Breaking Through, by Francisco Jimenez. IL: 5–8, YA; RL: 7.4. Having come from Mexico to California ten years earlier, fourteen-year-old Francisco is still working in the fields but fighting to improve his life and complete his education.

Carrot Seed, by Ruth Krauss. IL: K-3; RL: 2.2. Everyone tells a small boy that the carrot seed he has planted will never grow, but his patience is rewarded.

The Circuit, by Francisco Jimenez. IL: 5–8, YA; RL: 5.5. This story explores a migrant family's experiences moving through labor camps, facing poverty and impermanence, and discusses how they endure through faith, hope, and back-breaking work.

Eleanor, by Barbara Cooney. IL: K-3; RL: 4.2. Presents the difficult childhood of Eleanor Roosevelt, who suffered the loss of both parents and overcame shyness and loneliness.

The Goats, by Brock Cole. IL: 5–8, YA; RL: 5.8. Stripped and marooned on a small island by their fellow campers, a boy and a girl form an uneasy bond that grows into a deep friendship when they decide to run away and disappear without a trace.

Goin' Someplace Special, by Patricia Mckissack. IL: K-3; RL: 4.2. In segregated 1950s Nashville, a young African American girl braves a series of indignities and obstacles to get to one of the few integrated places in town: the public library.

Heat, by Mike Lupica. IL: 5–8; RL: 5.6. Pitching prodigy Michael Arroyo is on the run from social services after being banned from playing Little League baseball because rival coaches doubt he is only twelve years old and he has no parents to offer them proof.

Island of the Blue Dolphins, by Scott O'Dell. IL: 5–8; RL: 5.5. Left alone on a beautiful but isolated island off the coast of California, a young Indian girl spends eighteen years not only surviving through enormous courage and self-reliance, but finding a measure of happiness in her solitary life.

Julie of the Wolves, by Jean Craighead George. IL: 5–8; RL: 5.6. While running away from home and an unwanted marriage, a thirteen-year-old Eskimo girl becomes lost on the North Slope of Alaska and is befriended by a wolf pack.

A New Coat for Anna, by Harriet Ziefert. IL: K-3; RL: 2.0. Even though there is no money, Anna's mother finds a way to make Anna a badly needed winter coat.

Out of the Dust, by Karen Hesse. IL: 3–6; RL: 4.5. Fifteen-year-old Billie Jo relates the hardships of living on her family's wheat farm in Oklahoma during the dust bowl years of the Great Depression.

Ruby Holler, by Sharon Creech. IL: 3–6; RL: 6.0. Thirteen-year-old fraternal twins Dallas and Florida have grown up in a terrible orphanage, but their lives change forever when an eccentric but sweet older couple invites them on an adventure, beginning in an almost magical place called Ruby Holler.

Stone Fox, by John Reynolds Gardiner. IL: 3–6; RL: 4.7. Little Willie hopes to pay the back taxes on his grandfather's farm with the purse from a dog sled race he enters.

The Strength of Saints, by A. LaFaye. IL: 3–6; RL: 5.0. In 1936, fourteen-year-old Nissa takes a stand against racial prejudice and for her own integrity and independence, drawing on the support of her individualistic mother, her father and stepmother, and some of the inhabitants of their Louisiana town.

The Tale of Despereaux, by Kate DiCamillo. IL: 3–6; RL: 4.1. This story relates the adventures of Despereaux Tilling, a small mouse of unusual talents, the princess he loves, the servant girl who longs to be a princess, and a devious rat determined to bring them all to ruin.

Trouble Don't Last, by Shelley Pearsall. IL: 5–8; RL: 5.2. Samuel, an eleven-year-old Kentucky slave, and Harrison, the elderly slave who helped raise him, attempt to escape to Canada via the Underground Railroad.

When My Name Was Keoko, by Linda Sue Park. IL: 5–8, YA; RL: 5.7. With national pride and occasional fear, a brother and sister face the increasingly oppressive occupation of Korea by Japan during World War II, which threatens to suppress Korean culture entirely.

Proactivity

Alice in April, by Phyllis Reynolds Naylor. IL: 5–8; RL: 5.4. While trying to survive seventh grade, Alice discovers that turning thirteen years old will make her the Woman of the House at home, so she starts a campaign to get more appreciated for taking care of her father and older brother.

Catwings, by Ursula Le Guin. IL: 3–6; RL: 4.5. Four young cats with wings leave the city slums in search of a safe place to live. They finally meet two children with kind hands.

The Chocolate War, by Robert Cormier. IL: YA; RL: 6.0. Jerry Renault is forced into a psychological showdown with Trinity School's gang leader, Archie Costello, for refusing to be bullied into selling chocolates for its annual fundraising.

Darby, by Jonathon Scott. Fuqua. IL: 5–8; RL: 5.0. In 1926, nine-year-old Darby Carmichael stirs up trouble in Marlboro County, South Carolina, when she writes a story for the local newspaper promoting racial equality.

Elbert's Bad Word, by Audry Wood. IL: K-3; RL: 2.5. After shocking the guests at the elegant garden party by using a bad word, Elbert learns some acceptable substitutes from a helpful wizard.

Flush, by Carl Hiaasen. IL: 5–8; RL: 5.0. With their father jailed for sinking a river boat, Noah Underwood and his younger sister, Abbey, must gather evidence that the owner of this floating casino is emptying his bilge tanks into the protected waters around their Florida Keys home.

The Gardener, by Sarah Stewart. IL: K-3; RL: 3.5. In a series of letters, Lydia Grace relates what happens when, after her father loses his job, she goes to live with her Uncle Jim in the city and takes her love for gardening with her.

The Giver, by Lois Lowry. IL: 5–8; RL: 6.8. Given his lifetime assignment at the Ceremony of Twelve, Jonas becomes the receiver of memories shared by only one other in his community and discovers the terrible truth about the society in which he lives.

Hoot, by Carl Hiaasen. IL: YA; RL: NR. Roy, who is new to his small Florida community, becomes involved in another boy's attempt to save a colony of burrowing owls from a proposed construction site.

Igraine the Brave, by Cornelia Funke. IL: 3–6; RL: 5.6. Translation of *Igraine Ohnefurcht*. The daughter of two magicians, twelve-year-old Igraine wants nothing more than to be a knight; and when their castle is attacked by a treacherous neighbor bent on stealing their singing magic books, Igraine has an opportunity to demonstrate her bravery.

Misfits, by James Howe. IL: 5–8; RL: 8.3. Four students who do not fit in at their small-town middle school decide to create a third party for the student council elections to represent all students who have ever been called names.

Mississippi Trial, 1955, by Chris Crowe. IL: 5–8; RL: 5.1. In Mississippi in 1955, a-sixteen-year old finds himself at odds with his grandfather over issues surrounding the kidnapping and murder of a fourteen-year-old African American from Chicago.

Miss Rumphius, by Barbara Cooney. IL: K-3; RL: 2.9. As a child, Great Aunt Alice Rumphius resolved that when she grew up, she would go to faraway places, live by the sea in her old age, and do something to make the world more beautiful. She does all those things, the last being the most difficult of all.

Nothing But the Truth, by Avi. IL: 7–10; RL: 6.9. A ninth grader's suspension for singing "The Star-Spangled Banner" during homeroom becomes a national news story.

Rules of the Road, by Joan Bauer. IL: YA; RL: NR. Sixteen-year-old Jenna gets a job driving the elderly owner of a chain of successful shoe stores from Chicago to Texas to confront the son who is trying to force her to retire. Along the way, Jenna hones her talents as a saleswoman and finds the strength to face her alcoholic father.

Seventeenth Swap, by Eloise McGraw. IL: 5–8; RL: 5.0. Having no money, a thirteen-year-old begins a series of swaps to get the child he babysits for a pair of cowboy boots.

Tangerine, by Edward Bloor. IL: YA; RL: NR. Twelve-year-old Paul, who lives in the shadow of his football hero brother, Erik, fights for the right to play soccer despite his near blindness. In the process, he slowly begins to remember the incident that damaged his eyesight.

True Confessions of Charlotte Doyle, by Avi. IL: 5–8; RL: 7.0. As the lone young lady on a transatlantic voyage in 1832, Charlotte learns that the captain is murderous and the crew rebellious.

Whale Talk, by Chris Crutcher. IL: YA; RL: NR. Intellectually and athletically gifted, TJ, a multiracial, adopted teenager, shuns organized sports and the athletes at his high school until he agrees to form a swimming team and recruits some of the school's less popular students.

Where the Lilies Bloom, by Vera and William Cleaver. IL: 5–8; RL: 5.5. In the Great Smoky Mountains region, a fourteen-year-old girl struggles to keep her family together after their father dies.

Where the Red Fern Grows, by Wilson Rawls. IL: 5–8; RL: 5.2. A young boy living in the Ozarks achieves his heart's desire when he becomes the owner of two redbone hounds and teaches them to be champion hunters.

Whipping Boy, by Sid Fleischman. IL: 3–6; RL: 4.8. A bratty prince and his whipping boy have many adventures when they inadvertently trade places after becoming involved with dangerous outlaws.

Goal Setting

Abel's Island, by William Steig. IL: 3–6; RL: 5.5. Cast away on an uninhabited island, Abel, a very civilized mouse, finds his resourcefulness and endurance tested to the limit as he struggles to survive and return to his home.

Absolutely True Diary of a Part-Time Indian, by Sherman Alexie. IL: YA; RL: 8.8. Budding cartoonist Junior leaves his troubled school on the Spokane Indian Reservation to attend an all-white farm town school, where the only other Native American is the school mascot.

Alia's Mission: Saving the Books of Iraq, by Mark Alan Stamaty. IL: 5–8, RL: 6.5. Inspired by a true story. Presents the story of Alia, a librarian who lives and works in Basra, and her desperate attempt to save the books in the central library at the start of the Iraqi war in 2003.

Are You My Mother? by P. D. Eastman. IL: K-3; RL: 1.5. When a baby bird hatches while his mother is out searching for food, he leaves the nest for a series of adventures to try to determine his mother's identity.

Bloody Jack, by L. A. Meyer. IL: 5–8; RL: 6.9. Reduced to begging and thievery in the streets of London, a thirteen-year-old orphan disguises herself as a boy and connives her way onto a British warship set for high-sea adventure in search of pirates.

Brave Irene, by William Steig. IL: K-3; RL: 3.5. Plucky Irene, a dressmaker's daughter, braves a fierce snowstorm to deliver a new gown to the duchess in time for the ball.

Breaking Through, by Francisco Jimenez. IL: 5–8, YA; RL: 7.4. Having come from Mexico to California ten years earlier, fourteen-year-old Francisco is still working in the fields but fighting to improve his life and complete his education.

Bremen Town Musicians, by Ilse Plume. IL: K-3; RL: 4.6. This is a retelling of the Grimm tale in which an old donkey, dog, cat, and rooster, no longer wanted by their masters, set out for Bremen to become musicians.

Chair for My Mother, by Vera B. Williams. IL: K-3; RL: 3.8. A child, her waitress mother, and her grandmother save dimes to buy a comfortable armchair after all their furniture is lost in a fire.

Dogsong, by Gary Paulsen. IL: YA; RL: 5.8. A fourteen-year-old Eskimo boy who feels assailed by the modernity of his life takes a fourteen-hundred-mile journey by dog sled across ice, tundra, and mountains seeking his own song of himself.

Frog and Toad Together, by Arnold Lobel. IL: K-3; RL: 2.3. Five further adventures of two best friends as they share cookies, plant a garden, and test their bravery.

Herbie Jones, by Suzy Kline. IL: 3–6; RL: 4.2. Herbie's experiences in the third grade include finding bones in the boys' bathroom, wandering away from his class on their field trip, and being promoted to a higher reading group.

Higher Power of Lucky, by Susan Patron. IL: 3–6; RL: 5.8. Fearing that her legal guardian plans to abandon her to return to France, ten-year-old aspiring scientist Lucky Trimble determines to run away while also continuing to seek the higher power that will bring stability to her life.

Incredible Journey, by Sheila Burnford. IL: 5–8; RL: 6.5. A doughty young Labrador retriever, a roguish bull terrier, and an indomitable Siamese cat set out through the Canadian wilderness to make their way home to the family they love.

Ironman, by Chris Crutcher. IL: YA; RL: 6.8. While training for a triathlon, seventeen-year-old Bo attends an anger management group at school, which leads him to examine his relationship with his father.

Junebug, by Alice Mead. IL: 3–6; RL: 5.5. An inquisitive young boy who lives with his mother and younger sister in a rough housing project in New Haven, Connecticut, approaches his tenth birthday with a mixture of anticipation and worry.

The Little Engine That Could, by Watty Piper. IL: K-3; RL: 2.9. Although he is not very big, the Little Blue Engine agrees to try to pull a stranded train full of toys over the mountain.

Make Lemonade, by Virginia Euwer Wolff. IL: 7–10; RL: 5.2. In order to earn money for college, fourteen-year-old LaVaughn babysits for a teenage mother.

Midwife's Apprentice, by Karen Cushman. IL: YA; RL: NR. In medieval England, a nameless, homeless girl is taken in by a sharp-tempered midwife. In spite of obstacles and hardship, she eventually gains the three things she most wants: a full belly, a contented heart, and a place in this world.

Single Shard, by Linda Sue Park. IL: 5–8; RL: 6.7. Tree-ear, a thirteen-year-old orphan in medieval Korea, lives under a bridge in a potters' village and longs to learn how to throw the delicate celadon ceramics himself.

Staying Fat for Sarah Byrnes, by Chris Crutcher. IL: YA; RL: NR. The daily class discussions about the nature of man, the existence of God, abortion, organized religion, suicide, and other contemporary issues serve as a backdrop for a high school senior's attempt to answer a friend's dramatic cry for help.

The Tale of Despereaux, by Kate DiCamillo. IL: 3–6; RL: 4.1 This story relates the adventures of Despereaux Tilling, a small mouse of unusual talents, the princess he loves, the servant girl who longs to be a princess, and a devious rat determined to bring them all to ruin.

View from Saturday, by E. L. Konigsburg. IL: 3–6; RL: 4.8. Four students, with their own individual stories, develop a special bond and attract the attention of their teacher, a paraplegic, who chooses them to represent their sixth-grade class in the Academic Bowl competition.

Watership Down, by Richard Adams. IL: YA; RL: NR. Chronicles the adventures of a group of rabbits searching for a safe place to establish a new warren where they can live in peace.

Support Systems

Al Capone Does My Shirts, by Gennifer Choldenko. IL: 5–8; RL: 4.8. A twelve-year-old boy named Moose moves to Alcatraz Island in 1935, when prison guards' families were housed there, and has to contend with his extraordinary new environment in addition to life with his autistic sister.

Amber Was Brave, Essie Was Smart, by Vera B. Williams. IL: 3–6; RL: 5.4. A series of poems tells how two sisters help each other deal with life while their mother is working and their father has been sent to jail.

A Brief Chapter in My Impossible Life, by Dana Reinhardt. IL: YA. Sixteen-year-old atheist Simone Turner-Bloom's life changes in unexpected ways when her parents convince her to make contact with her biological mother, an agnostic from a Jewish family who is losing her battle with cancer.

Charlotte's Web, by E. B. White. IL: 3–6; RL: 4.0. Wilbur the pig is desolate when he discovers that he is destined to be the farmer's Christmas dinner until his spider friend, Charlotte, decides to help him.

The Cricket in Times Square, by George Selden. IL: 3–6; RL: 6.2. A country cricket unintentionally arrives in New York, where he is befriended by Tucker Mouse and Harry Cat.

Fig Pudding, by Ralph Fletcher. IL: 3–6; RL: 4.9. Cliff describes the excitement, conflict, and sudden tragedy that his large and boisterous family experiences during his eleventh year.

The Flunking of Joshua T. Bates, by Susan Shreve. IL: 3–6; RL: 3.2. Driving home from the beach on Labor Day, Joshua receives some shocking news from his mother: he must repeat third grade.

Freak the Mighty, by Rodman Philbrick. IL: 5–8; RL: 6.3. At the beginning of eighth grade, Max, who has learning disabilities, and his new friend, Freak, whose birth defect has affected his body but not his brilliant mind, find that when they combine forces, they make a powerful team.

Frog and Toad Are Friends, by Arnold Lobel. IL: K-3; RL: 2.4. Five tales recounting the adventures of two best friends: Frog and Toad.

Gossie and Gertie, by Olivier Dunrea. IL: K-3; RL: 2.5. Gossie and Gertie are best friends, and everywhere Gossie goes, Gertie goes too, except when she doesn't, and sometimes that's even better.

Granny Torrelli Makes Soup, by Sharon Creech. IL: 3–6; RL: 4.5. With the help of her wise old grandmother, twelve-year-old Rosie manages to work out some problems in her relationship with her best friend, Bailey, the boy next door.

Ironman, by Chris Crutcher. IL: YA; RL: 6.8. While training for a triathlon, seventeen-year-old Bo attends an anger management group at school, which leads him to examine his relationship with his father.

Jericho Walls, by Kristi Collier. IL: 5–8; RL: 5.8 In 1957, when her preacher father accepts a post in Jericho, Alabama, Jo wants to fit in, but her growing friendship with a black boy forces her to confront the racism of the South and reconsider her own values.

Loser, by Jerry Spinelli. IL: 3–6; RL: 5.2. Although Daniel Zinkoff's classmates since first grade have considered him strange and a loser, his optimism and exuberance, and the support of his loving family, do not allow him to feel that way about himself.

Mouse and His Child, by Russell Hoban. IL: 3–6; RL: 5.8. Two discarded toy mice survive perilous adventures in a hostile world before finding security and happiness with old friends and new.

Mrs. Frisby and the Rats of NIMH, by Robert C. O'Brien. IL: 3–6; RL: 5.8. Having no one to help her with her problems, a widowed mouse visits the rats whose former imprisonment in a laboratory has made them wise and long-lived.

River Between Us, by Richard Peck. IL: YA; RL: NR. During the early days of the Civil War, the Pruitt family takes in two mysterious young ladies who have fled New Orleans to come north to Illinois.

Same Stuff as Stars, by Katherine Patterson. IL: 5–8; RL: 5.4. When Angel's self-absorbed mother leaves her and her younger brother with their poor great-grandmother, the eleven-year-old girl worries not only about her mother and brother, her imprisoned father, and the frail old woman, but also about a mysterious man who begins sharing with her the wonder of the stars.

Seedfolks, by Paul Fleischman. IL: 5–8; RL: 5.0. One by one, people of varying ages and backgrounds transform a trash-filled inner-city lot into a productive and beautiful garden. In doing so, the gardeners themselves are transformed.

Surviving the Applewhites, by Stephanie Tolan. IL: 5–8, YA; RL: 5.7. Jake, a budding juvenile delinquent, is sent for home schooling to the arty and eccentric Applewhite family's Creative Academy, where he discovers talents and interests he never knew he had.

Thank You Mr. Falker, by Patricia Polacco. IL: K-3; RL: 4.8 At first, Trisha loves school, but her difficulty learning to read makes her feel dumb, until, in the fifth grade, a new teacher helps her understand and overcome her problem.

What Would Joey Do? by Jack Gantos. IL: 5–8; RL: 6.2 Joey tries to keep his life from degenerating into total chaos when his mother sends him to be home-schooled with a hostile blind girl, his divorced parents cannot stop fighting, and his grandmother is dying of emphysema.

When the Circus Came to Town, by Laurence Yep. IL: 3–6; RL: 5.7. An Asian cook and a Chinese New Year celebration help a ten-year-old girl at a Montana stagecoach station regain her confidence after smallpox scars her face.

Zen Ties, by Jon Muth. IL: K–3/ RL: 1.9. When Stillwater the panda encourages Koo, Addy, Michael, and Karl to help a grouchy neighbor, their efforts are rewarded in unexpected ways.

Emotional Coping Strategies

Because of Winn-Dixie, by Kate DiCamillo. IL: 3–6; RL: 5.8. Ten-year-old India Opal Buloni describes her first summer in the town of Naomi, Florida, and all the good things that happen to her because of her big, ugly dog, Winn-Dixie.

The Book Thief, by Markus Zusak. IL: YA; RL: N/A. Trying to make sense of the horrors of World War II, Death relates the story of Liesel: a young German girl whose book-stealing and storytelling talents help sustain her family and the Jewish man they are hiding, as well as their neighbors.

Buddha Boy, by Kathe Koja. IL: 5–8; RL: 7.2. Justin spends time with Jinsen, the unusual and artistic new student whom the school bullies torment and call Buddha Boy. Justin ends up making choices that have an impact on Jinsen, himself, and the entire school.

Corner of the Universe, by Ann Martin. IL: 5–8; RL: 7.3. The summer that Hattie turns twelve, she meets the childlike uncle she never knew and becomes friends with a girl who works at the carnival that comes to Hattie's small town.

The Day No Pigs Would Die, by Robert Newton Peck. IL: 5–8; RL: 5.0. To a thirteen-year-old Vermont farm boy whose father slaughters pigs for a living, maturity comes early as he learns "doing what's got to be done," especially regarding his pet pig who cannot produce a litter.

Dear Mr. Henshaw, by Beverly Cleary. IL: 3–6; RL: 5.0. In his letters to his favorite author, ten-year-old Leigh reveals his problems in coping with his parents' divorce, being the new boy in school, and generally finding his own place in the world.

Did I Ever Tell You How Lucky You Are, by Dr. Seuss. IL: K–3; RL: 3.5. Compared to the problems of some of the creatures the old man describes, the boy is really quite lucky.

Each Little Bird that Sings, by Deborah Wiles. IL: 3–6; RL: 4.0. Comfort Snowberger is well acquainted with death, since her family runs the funeral parlor in their small southern town. Even so, the ten-year-old is unprepared for the series of heart-wrenching events that begins on the first day of Easter vacation with the sudden death of her beloved Great-Uncle Edisto.

Hole in My Life, by Jack Gantos. IL: YA; RL: NR. The author relates how, as a young adult, he became a drug user and smuggler, was arrested, did time in prison, and eventually got out and went to college, all the while hoping to become a writer.

How I Became a Writer and Oggie Learned to Drive, by Janet Taylor Lisle. IL: 3–6; RL: 6.8. As sixth-grader Archie and his six-year-old brother, Oggie, shuttle back and forth between their separated parents' two homes, Archie tries desperately to take care of Oggie and to pretend that everything is normal.

Jim Ugly, by Sid Fleischman. IL: 3–6; RL: 5.8. Adventures surround twelve-year-old Jake and Jim Ugly, his father's part-mongrel, part-wolf dog, as they travel through the Old West trying to find out what really happened to Jake's actor father.

Kami and the Yaks, by Andrea Stenn Stryer. IL: K–3; RL: 2.6. Kami, a young, deaf Sherpa boy, sets off on his own to find his family's missing yaks and finds one of them caught between rocks. But when he runs home to get help from his family, he has trouble at first being understood.

Pictures of Hollis Woods, by Patricia Reilly Giff. IL: YA; RL: NR. A troublesome twelve-year-old orphan, staying with an elderly artist who needs her, remembers the only other time she was happy in a foster home, with a family that truly seemed to care about her.

Sees Behind Trees, by Michael Dorris. IL: 3–6; RL: 5.9. A Native American boy with a special gift to "see" beyond his poor eyesight journeys with an old warrior to a land of mystery and beauty.

Spinky Sulks, by William Steig. IL: K-3; RL: 2.8. Spinky believes his family does not love him or understand him, and nothing they say will convince him otherwise.

Stand Tall, by Joan Bauer. IL: 5–8; RL: 6.9. Tree, a six-foot, three-inch twelve-year-old, copes with his parents' recent divorce and his failure as an athlete by helping his grandfather, a Vietnam vet and recent amputee, and Sophie, a new girl at school.

Stoner and Spaz, by Ron Koertge. IL: YA; RL: NR. A troubled youth with cerebral palsy struggles toward self-acceptance with the help of a drug-addicted young woman.

Stop Pretending, by Sonya Sones. IL: 5–8, YA; RL: 5.0. A younger sister has a difficult time adjusting to life after her older sister has a mental breakdown.

Tar Beach, by Faith Ringgold. IL: K-3; RL: 4.4. A young girl dreams of flying above her Harlem home, claiming all she sees for herself and her family. The book is based on the author's quilt painting of the same name.

That Summer, by Tony Johnston. IL: K-3; RL: 3.6. A family, including a child who is dying, together sews a quilt of its memories and love.

Velveteen Rabbit, by Margery Williams Bianco. IL: K-3; RL: 4.8. By the time the Velveteen Rabbit is dirty, worn out, and about to be burned, he has almost given up hope of ever finding the magic called Real.

Wenny Has Wings, by Janet Lee Carey. IL: 3–6; RL: 4.6. Having had a near-death experience in the accident that killed his younger sister, eleven-year-old Will tries to cope with the situation by writing her letters.

Movies

Movies can be used in much the same way as books for teaching about the Success Attributes. Presenting stories through sight and sound can be an excellent format for students with reading problems. Movies might be used in place of books or as an accompanying format. Depending on the specific circumstance, setting, and purpose, movies may be shown in their entirety or limited to particular scenes, sections, or clips. The same basic guidelines for selecting and using books apply to movies.

The movies in the following list are illustrative of one or more Success Attributes. Some movies include characters struggling with disabilities, and others do not. Movie ratings are provided as available. The list is in no way intended to be exhaustive. Rather, it is a sampling of movies that may help students understand and develop the success attributes.

Movies are listed in alphabetical order with the pertinent Success Attribute designated.

An American Tail (1986). This beautifully rendered animated film tells an overly familiar story in terms children can easily understand. Fievel Mousekewitz and his family of Russian-Jewish mice escape from their homeland in the late 1800s, boarding a boat headed toward America to evade the czarist rule of the Russian cats. Upon his arrival in New York City, Fievel is separated from his family and discovers to his horror that there are cats in America too (his father said there weren't). Fievel meets his share of friendly and hostile mice, and he eventually befriends a cat as well. Rating: Not rated. *Success Attributes:* Self-Awareness, Perseverance, Use of Social Support Systems.

Annie (1999). This is a charming tale of an adorable orphan named Annie. For a young girl living a "hard-knock" life in a children's orphanage, things can seem pretty bad, especially at Christmas. But feisty Annie carries a song in her heart and hope in her locket, the only thing she has from her parents. One day, fed up with the dastardly Miss Hannigan, Annie escapes the rundown orphanage, determined to find her mom and dad. Her adventure takes her from the cold, mean streets of New York to the warm, comforting arms of big-hearted billionaire Oliver Warbucks, with plenty of mischief and music in between. Categories: Musical, children's/family. Rating: Not rated. *Success Attributes:* Perseverance, Proactivity, Emotional Coping Strategies, Use of Social Support Systems.

Benny and June (1993). This is a wonderfully unique and delightfully offbeat romantic comedy. Joon is a little unbalanced. Sometimes, without warning, her sweet nature gives way to odd behavior, including a penchant for setting fires. She lives with her older brother, Benny, who has spent his life taking care of her since their parents died. One night, while playing in a poker game with unusual stakes, Joon loses her hand—and wins Sam, a whimsical misfit who soon charms his way into her heart. Now if they could only find the perfect mate for her overprotective brother. Categories: Comedy, romance. Rating: PG. *Success Attributes:* Self-Awareness, Use of Social Support Systems, Emotional Coping Strategies.

Breaking Away (1979). Teenagers adapt to life after high school in this low-key, acclaimed, bittersweet comedy-drama. This amiable sleeper remains joyous fare for those seeking colorful, endearing characters and a realistic drama with comic undertones. Categories: Comedy, drama. Rating: PG. *Success Attribute:* Perseverance.

Door to Door (2002, TV movie). This movie is based on the true story of Bill Porter, a man who suffered from the effects of cerebral palsy, spoke with difficulty, had severe spinal problems that caused him to walk in a stooped manner, and who was not blessed with good looks. Despite all of these apparent strikes against him, Bill Porter was blessed with an indomitable spirit and drive to succeed on his own. Category: Drama. Rating: Not rated. *Success Attributes:* Perseverance, Proactivity, Goal Setting.

Freaky Friday (2003). A mother and teenage daughter disagree about everything. After a magical switch, they inhabit each other's bodies and learn to respect each other's viewpoint. *Success Attribute:* Self-Awareness

Finding Nemo (2003). Father-and-son clownfish, Marlin and Nemo, become separated in the Great Barrier Reef, and little Nemo ends up in a fish tank in dentist's office. Grief stricken, Marlin goes on a wild adventure to find and rescue his son. Categories: Animation, comedy, children's. Rating: G. *Success Attributes:* Perseverance, Self-Awareness, Emotional Coping Strategies, Use of Social Support Systems.

Forrest Gump (1994). This all-American social drama follows a simple but honorable man as he unwittingly influences some of the most important people and events from the 1950s to the 1970s in U.S. history, including Elvis Presley, John Kennedy, Lyndon Johnson, Richard Nixon, and the war in Vietnam, all while carrying a torch for his beloved Jenny. Categories: Comedy, drama. Rating: PG-13. *Success Attributes:* Perseverance, Use of Social Support Systems, Goal Setting.

Ice Age (2002). Energetic, computer-animated, prehistoric-era buddy comedy relates the adventures of a mammoth and sloth that find a human infant and are forced to rely on the help of a shifty saber-tooth tiger to return the baby to its tribe. Categories: Fantasy, children's/family. Rating: PG. *Success Attributes:* Use of Social Support Systems, Perseverance.

The Miracle Worker (1962). This is an uplifting true story about a deaf, blind, and mute girl as she learns to communicate with the world. Categories: Drama, family. Rating: Not rated. *Success Attributes:* Perseverance, Self-Awareness, Use of Social Support Systems, Goal Setting.

October Sky (1999). This emotionally uplifting crowd pleaser shows teenagers in a 1950s mining town intent on building a rocket. Categories: Drama, family. Rating: PG. *Success*

Attributes: Self-Awareness, Perseverance, Proactivity, Goal Setting Use of Social Support Systems.

Stand and Deliver (1988). This is a true tale of a tough teacher who motivates a class of potential losers into realizing amazing achievements. Category: Drama. Rating: PG. *Success Attributes:* Use of Social Support Systems, Perseverance, Self-Awareness.

To Kill a Mockingbird (1962). This compelling classic confronts racial bigotry through the tale of a widowed southern lawyer and his children. Sensitive coming-of-age tales and riveting courtroom confrontations. Categories: Drama, classic. Rating: Not rated. *Success Attributes:* Use of Social Support Systems, Self-Awareness, Perseverance, Proactivity.

Related Books, Articles, and Curricula

Books

Brooks, R., & Goldstein, S. (2001). *Raising resilient children.* New York: McGraw-Hill.

Roffman, A. J. (2000). *Meeting the challenge of learning disabilities in adulthood.* Baltimore, MD: Paul H. Brookes.

Shure, M. B. (2000). *Raising a thinking preteen: The "I can problem solve" program for 8-to-12-year-olds.* New York: Holt.

Articles

Cosden, M., Brown, C., & Elliott, K. (2002). Development of self-understanding and self-esteem in children and adults with learning disabilities. In B. Wong & M. L. Donahue (Eds.), *The social dimensions of learning disabilities: Essays in honor of Tanis Bryan* (pp. 33–50). Mahwah, NJ: Erlbaum.

Reiff, H. B., Gerber, P. J., & Ginsberg, R. (1994). Instructional strategies for long-term success. *Annals of Dyslexia, 44,* 272–288.

Roffman, A., Herzog, J., & Wershba, P. (1994). Helping young adults understand their learning disabilities. *Journal of Learning Disabilities, 27,* 413–419.

Wehmeyer, M. L. (1996). Student self-report measure of self-determination for students with cognitive disabilities. *Education and Training in Mental Retardation and Developmental Disabilities, 31,* 282–293.

Curricula

Field, S., & Hoffman, A. (1996). *Steps to self-determination: A curriculum to help adolescents learn to achieve their goals.* Austin, TX: Pro-Ed.

Field, S., Martin, J., Miller, R., Ward, M., & Wehmeyer, M. (1998). *A practical guide for teaching self-determination.* Reston, VA: Council for Exceptional Children.

Gold, E., & Sheets, D. (2003). *My future plan: A transition notebook to help you plan your life after high school.* Washington, DC: State of the Art.

Appendix B: Assessments

The checklists follow the same format but have different purposes. An individual (teacher or student) may use the first set of checklists: the Individual Self-Assessment. If these are completed several times over the year, progress may be monitored by comparing and contrasting responses from one time to the next. The second list (the Class Record of Progress) allows the teacher to code the progress of members of a class. The teacher may record students' names in the boxes at the top and then supply a code (numbers, checks or pluses) to evaluate how students in a class are succeeding through the attributes. Either one or the other checklist may be of assistance to the teacher for organizing students' work through the attributes.

Individual Self-Assessment
Self-Awareness

	Strongly Agree			Neutral			Strongly Disagree
Is aware of his or her academic strengths	❏	❏	❏	❏	❏	❏	❏
Is aware of his or her academic weaknesses	❏	❏	❏	❏	❏	❏	❏
Is aware of his or her nonacademic strengths	❏	❏	❏	❏	❏	❏	❏
Is aware of his or her nonacademic weaknesses	❏	❏	❏	❏	❏	❏	❏
Is aware of his or her special talents and abilities	❏	❏	❏	❏	❏	❏	❏
Is aware of his or her feelings, opinions, and values	❏	❏	❏	❏	❏	❏	❏
Is able to match activities to strengths	❏	❏	❏	❏	❏	❏	❏
Understands his or her specific learning disability	❏	❏	❏	❏	❏	❏	❏
Accepts his or her learning disability	❏	❏	❏	❏	❏	❏	❏
Is able to compartmentalize	❏	❏	❏	❏	❏	❏	❏
Uses strategies to work around the learning disability	❏	❏	❏	❏	❏	❏	❏

Proactivity

	Strongly Agree			Neutral			Strongly Disagree
Participates in classroom and extracurricular social activities	❑	❑	❑	❑	❑	❑	❑
Makes decisions and acts on those decisions	❑	❑	❑	❑	❑	❑	❑
Understands the advantages and disadvantages of making certain decisions	❑	❑	❑	❑	❑	❑	❑
Recognizes when a decision needs to be made	❑	❑	❑	❑	❑	❑	❑
Knows how to evaluate decisions	❑	❑	❑	❑	❑	❑	❑
Takes responsibility for his or her actions	❑	❑	❑	❑	❑	❑	❑
Feels he or she has control over his or her world	❑	❑	❑	❑	❑	❑	❑
Is assertive and stands up for self	❑	❑	❑	❑	❑	❑	❑
Is self-confident	❑	❑	❑	❑	❑	❑	❑

Perseverance

	Strongly Agree			Neutral			Strongly Disagree
Understands the benefits of perseverance	❑	❑	❑	❑	❑	❑	❑
Keeps working at academic tasks despite difficulties	❑	❑	❑	❑	❑	❑	❑
Keeps working at nonacademic tasks despite difficulties	❑	❑	❑	❑	❑	❑	❑
Knows how to deal with obstacles and setbacks	❑	❑	❑	❑	❑	❑	❑
Knows how to adjust to change	❑	❑	❑	❑	❑	❑	❑
Knows when to quit	❑	❑	❑	❑	❑	❑	❑

	Strongly Agree			Neutral			Strongly Disagree
Sets academic goals	❑	❑	❑	❑	❑	❑	❑
Sets nonacademic goals	❑	❑	❑	❑	❑	❑	❑
Can prioritize goals	❑	❑	❑	❑	❑	❑	❑
Knows when a goal is realistic	❑	❑	❑	❑	❑	❑	❑
Develops plans or steps for reaching goals	❑	❑	❑	❑	❑	❑	❑
Understands the relationship between short- and long-term goals	❑	❑	❑	❑	❑	❑	❑
Finds alternative ways to reach goals when faced with obstacles	❑	❑	❑	❑	❑	❑	❑
Understands the need to work with others to reach goals	❑	❑	❑	❑	❑	❑	❑

Presence and Use of Effective Support Systems

	Strongly Agree			Neutral			Strongly Disagree
Knows when he or she needs help	❑	❑	❑	❑	❑	❑	❑
Knows how to get help	❑	❑	❑	❑	❑	❑	❑
Seeks help when needed	❑	❑	❑	❑	❑	❑	❑
Is willing to use technological supports	❑	❑	❑	❑	❑	❑	❑
Is aware of laws to help persons with learning disabilities	❑	❑	❑	❑	❑	❑	❑

Emotional Coping Strategies

	Strongly Agree			Neutral			Strongly Disagree
Is aware of how his or her emotional reactions affect behavior	❑	❑	❑	❑	❑	❑	❑
Is aware of situations that cause stress, frustration, and emotional upset	❑	❑	❑	❑	❑	❑	❑
Has developed strategies for avoiding or reducing stress	❑	❑	❑	❑	❑	❑	❑
Is able to recognize the onset of stress	❑	❑	❑	❑	❑	❑	❑
Knows when outside support/help is needed	❑	❑	❑	❑	❑	❑	❑

Class Record of Progress

TEACHER: _____

Student Name														
Self-Awareness														
Is aware of his or her academic strengths														
Is aware of his or her academic weaknesses														
Is aware of his or her nonacademic strengths														
Is aware of his or her nonacademic weaknesses														
Is aware of his or her special talents and abilities														
Is aware of his or her feelings, opinions, and values														
Is able to match activities to strengths														
Understands his or her specific learning disability														
Accepts his or her learning disability														
Is able to compartmentalize														
Uses strategies to work around the learning disability														
Proactivity														
Participates in classroom and extracurricular social activities														

TEACHER:_____

Student Name														
Makes decisions and acts on those decisions														
Understands the advantages and disadvantages of making certain decisions														
Recognizes when a decision needs to be made														
Knows how to evaluate decisions														
Takes responsibility for his or her actions														
Feels he or she has control over his or her world														
Is assertive and stands up for self														
Is self-confident														
Perseverance														
Understands the benefits of perseverance														
Keeps working at academic tasks despite difficulties														
Keeps working at nonacademic tasks despite difficulties														
Knows how to deal with obstacles and setbacks														
Knows how to adjust to change														
Knows when to quit														

TEACHER:_____

Student Name													
Goal Setting													
Sets academic goals													
Sets nonacademic goals													
Can prioritize goals													
Knows when a goal is realistic													
Develops plans and steps for reaching goals													
Understands the relationship between short- and long-term goals													
Finds alternative ways to reach goals when faced with obstacles													
Understands the need to work with others to reach goals													
Presence and Use of Effective Support Systems													
Knows when he or she needs help													
Knows how to get help													
Seeks help when needed													
Is willing to use technological supports													
Is aware of laws to help persons with learning disabilities													
Emotional Coping Strategies													

TEACHER:_____

Student Name													
Is aware of how his or her emotional reactions affect behavior													
Is aware of situations that cause stress, frustration, and emotional upset													
Has developed strategies for avoiding or reducing stress													
Is able to recognize the onset of stress													
Knows when outside support or help is needed													

References

Aiex, N. K. (1993). *Bibliotherapy*. (Report No. EDO-CS-93–05). Bloomington: Indiana University, Office of Educational Research and Improvement. (ERIC Document Reproduction Service No. ED 357333)

Forgan, J. W. (2002). Using bibliotherapy to teach problem solving. *Intervention in School and Clinic, 38*(2), 75–82.

Goldberg, R. J., Higgins, E. L., Raskind, M. H., & Herman, K. L. (2003). Predictors of success in individuals with learning disabilities: A qualitative analysis of a 20-year longitudinal study. *Learning Disabilities Research and Practice, 18*(4), 222–236.

Higgins, E. L., Raskind, M. H., Goldberg, R. J., & Herman, K. L. (2002). Stages of acceptance of a learning disability: The impact of labeling. *Learning Disability Quarterly, 25*, 3–18.

Hildreth, B. L., & Candler, A. (1992). Learning about learning disabilities through general public literature. *Intervention in School and Clinic, 27*(5), 293–296.

Raskind, M. H., Goldberg, R. J., Higgins, E. L., & Herman, K. L. (2002). Teaching "life success" to students with learning disabilities: Lessons learned from a 20-year study. *Intervention in School and Clinic, 37*(4), 201–208.

Raskind, M. H., Goldberg, R. J., Higgins, E. L., & Herman, K. L. (1999). Patterns of change and predictors of success in individuals with learning disabilities: Results from a twenty-year longitudinal study. *Learning Disabilities Research and Practice, 14*(1), 35–49.

Spekman, N. J., Goldberg, R. J., & Herman K. L. (1992). Learning disabled children grow up: A search for factors related to success in the young adult years. *Learning Disabilities Research and Practice, 7*, 161–170.

Sridhar, D., & Vaughn, S. (2000). Bibliotherapy for all: Enhancing reading comprehension, self-concept, and behavior. *Teaching Exceptional Children, 33*(2), 74–82.

Tu, W. (1999). *Using literature to help children cope with problems*. (Report No. EDO-CS-99–09). Bloomington, IN: ERIC Clearinghouse on Reading, English, and Communication (ERIC Document Reproduction Service No. ED 436008)

Index

W